Landmarks of world literature

Ezra Pound

THE CANTOS

Landmarks of world literature

General Editor: J. P. Stern

EZRA POUND

The Cantos

GEORGE KEARNS

Rutgers University

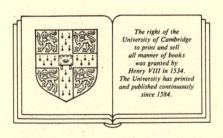

The right of the
University of Cambridge
to print and sell
all manner of books
was granted by
Henry VIII in 1534.
The University has printed
and published continuously
since 1584.

CAMBRIDGE UNIVERSITY PRESS

Cambridge
New York *Port Chester*
Melbourne *Sydney*

Published by the Press Syndicate of the University of Cambridge
The Pitt Building, Trumpington Street, Cambridge CB2 1RP
32 West 57th Street, New York, NY 10022, USA
10 Stamford Road, Oakleigh, Melbourne 3166, Australia

First published 1989

Printed in Great Britain at the University Press, Cambridge

British Library cataloguing in publication data

Kearns, George
Ezra Pound: the Cantos. – (Landmarks in world
literature).
1. Literature. Criticism. Pound, Ezra, 1885–1972 –
Critical studies
I. Title II. Series
811′.52

Library of Congress cataloguing in publication data

Kearns, George.
Ezra Pound. The cantos / George Kearns.
    p.   cm. – (Landmarks of world literature)
Bibliography.
ISBN 0–521–33373–3. – ISBN 0–521–33649–x (pbk.)
1. Pound, Ezra, 1885–1972. Cantos. I. Title.
PS3531.082C2858 1989
811′.52 – dc20 89–1043 CIP

ISBN 0 521 33373 3 hard covers
ISBN 0 521 33649 X paperback

Contents

v

Preface

My aim in this brief introduction to Pound's *Cantos* — brief
for a poem of 800 pages, each of which is a centrifugal force
spinning off pages of explication — is to address the reader
approaching the poem for the first time. I have tried to con-
vey a sense of what the poem is about, and of its aesthetic and
political–ethical–didactic dimensions. There are detailed
demonstrations of the complex, often curious activities one
performs while "reading" Pound. I have been acutely aware
of steering a course between the Scylla of making the poem
sound easier than it is, which can only lead to disappointment, and the Charybdis of making it appear so formidable
and arcane, so removed from the concerns of our lives, that
the reader will see no point in going on with it.

It is hoped that this study cannot be mis-read as a potted
version, something the reader — facing examinations, for
example — can substitute for time spent with the text. It
has been designed to resist such usage, such usury, for in
Poundian terms that sort of substitute reading would be like
collecting interest on someone else's money. T. S. Eliot, in an
introductory note to David Jones's *In Parenthesis*, a work he
thought had strong "affinities" with the *Cantos*, offers wise
advice:

Good commentaries can be very helpful: but to study even the best
commentary on a work of literary art is likely to be a waste of time
unless we have first read and been excited by the text commented
upon even without understanding it. For that thrill of excitement
from our first reading of a work . . . which we do not understand
is itself the beginning of understanding. . . We must have the
experience before we attempt to explore the sources of the work
itself.

I assume the reader has at hand a copy of the complete

Cantos and will turn to many of the references, allowing the eye occasionally to wander off course. The Guide to further reading includes both works enthusiastic, pro-Pound, pro-*Cantos*, and works that take more qualified, sometimes severely disapproving views. Through them the reader may be introduced to advanced, sometimes sharp critical debates which the present study can only glance at.

The reader will find that I have many problems with, and objections to, the poetics and politics of the *Cantos*, yet it should be obvious that I wouldn't be writing at length about the poem if I did not think it greatly rewarding. While I have tried to avoid idiosyncratic interpretations, I make no pretense at neutral or "objective" stances, which could only be, to paraphrase a remark of Sterne's that Pound enjoyed, a mysterious carriage of the body to disguise the defects of ideology. For all my quarrels with him and with his poem, I am very fond of Pound. The spirit of this introduction to the poem may broadly be indicated by a note Pound wrote as he approached eighty:

in the rare cases when criticism helps a reader to understand a text, it is probably due to the critic's perception of positive values and to his not having looked for something which the author never intended to put into his work.

The early attacks on Keats, he continued, were "due in part to an incomprehension of why Keats could expect a thing of beauty to be a joy" (*CC* 322).

I wish to thank for their invaluable comments: the general editor, J. P. Stern; my friend, Derek Attridge; and my wife, Cleo McNelly Kearns, to whom this book is dedicated.

Abbreviations

References to the *Cantos* are by canto number and page number: (36/177). This has worked since 1976 with both Faber and New Directions editions; older Faber texts will show different page numbers as well as occasional variant readings. I have used the New Directions tenth printing (1986), which includes the two cantos written in Italian, 72 and 73, and a "Fragment (1966)"; this prints among the final fragments lines which appeared in some editions as Canto 120 ("I have tried to write Paradise"). References to Pound's works are abbreviated:

CC,	*Confucius to Cummings*
GB,	*Gaudier-Brzeska*
GK,	*Guide to Kulchur*
JM,	*Jefferson and/or Mussolini*
L,	*Selected Letters*
LE,	*Literary Essays*
PD,	*Pavannes and Divagations*
PF,	*Pound/Ford*
PL,	*Pound/Lewis*
PZ,	*Pound/Zukovsky*
SP,	*Selected Prose* − where pagination differs for *Selected Prose*, the page in the New Directions edition is first, in the Faber edition second and in italics: (*SP* 81:*95*).
SR,	*Spirit of Romance*

Articles in *Paideuma* are by volume, number, page: *Pai*, 15.2–3.111. All works mentioned may be located in the Guide to further reading.

ix

Chronology

	Ezra Pound's life and work	*Literary and cultural events*	*Historical events*
1885	Born at Hailey, Idaho	Marx, *Das Kapital*	Presidency of Grover Cleveland
1887	Family moves to New York	Nietzsche, *The Genealogy of Morals*	Queen Victoria's Golden Jubilee
1898	Family settles in Wyncote, a Philadelphia suburb	Hardy, *Wessex Poems*; H. G. Wells, *The War of the Worlds*	Spanish–American War; Spain cedes Puerto Rico, and the Philippines to the United States
1901	Attends University of Pennsylvania, begins lifelong friendships with H. D. [Hilda Doolittle] and William Carlos Williams	Kipling, *Kim*; Mann, *Buddenbrooks*; Strindberg, *Dance of Death*; Freud, *The Psychopathology of Everyday Life*	Boer War in South Africa; Socialist Revolution Party in Russia; strikes and anarchism in France and Italy
1903	At Hamilton College in New York State through 1905	James, *The Ambassadors*; Yeats, *In the Seven Woods*	Panama gains independence from Colombia with U.S. support
1905	Studies Romance languages at University of Pennsylvania; M.A. 1907	Conrad, *Nostromo*; Chekhov, *The Cherry Orchard*	Russian fleet destroyed in Japanese war; Japan emerges as world power
1907	Travels to Spain. Teaches Romance languages, Wabash College, Indiana. Dismissed after a scandal	Cubist paintings in Paris; Stein writing *The Making of Americans*; Picasso, *Les Demoiselles d'Avignon*	Suppression of liberal policies and dissent in Russia; European and American women agitate for vote
1908	Leaves for Europe. Publishes *A Lume Spento* at own expense. Moves to London. *A Quinzaine for this Yule*	T. E. Hulme discusses the "image"; Forster, *A Room With A View*; Brancusi, *The Kiss*	Growth of German Naval power; Taft defeats Bryan for presidency; Liberal government in Britain

Year			
1909	Meets Yeats, T. E. Hulme, Ford Madox Ford. Publishes *Personae* and *Exultations*	Marinetti, "Futurism"; Schoenberg, *Three Piano Pieces* ("atonal" music); Stein, *Three Lives*	Britain prepares to meet German naval build-up; Henry Ford develops "Model T" car
1910	*The Spirit of Romance* (prose)	Post-impressionist show in London	Japan annexes Korea
1911	*Canzoni*. Translates Cavalcanti. Begins writing for the *New Age*	Matisse, *The Red Studio*; Forster, *Howards End*	Suffragette riots and dock strikes in London
1912	Invents "Imagism" (with H. D. and others). *Ripostes*. Meets Henry James. Begins association with Harriet Monroe's *Poetry* (Chicago)	Futurist exhibition in London; Duchamps, *Nude Descending a Staircase*; Stravinski, *Petrushka*	Woodrow Wilson elected; last Manchu emperor abdicates in China; Minimum Wage Bill in Britain after miners' strike
1913	Meets the sculptor, Gaudier-Brzeska. Close association with Yeats. First contact with Joyce. Works with Fenollosa manuscripts on Chinese poetry and Japanese *Noh* plays	Armory Show of post-impressionist art in NY; Epstein, *Rock Drill*; Lawrence, *Sons and Lovers*; Proust, *Swann's Way*; Lewis, *Timon of Athens* (Vorticist graphics)	Balkan wars involve Russia, Bulgaria, Turkey, Greece, Serbia; Britain and France oppose German–Turkish military alliance; Panama canal completed
1914	Marries Dorothy Shakespear. *Des Imagistes* (anthology). Works with Wyndham Lewis on *Blast* and the Vorticist movement. Meets T. S. Eliot. Sends "Prufrock" to *Poetry*	James, *The Golden Bowl*; Joyce, *Dubliners*; serial publication of Joyce's *Portrait of the Artist*; Stein, *Tender Buttons*; Gaudier-Brzeska, *Birds Erect*	Austrian Archduke Ferdinand and wife assassinated in Sarajevo; World War begins in July; Britain, France, Germany, Austria–Hungary, Turkey and Russia in arms
1915	*Cathay* (Chinese translations from Fenollosa's notes). Begins work on the *Cantos*	Lawrence's *The Rainbow* suppressed in Britain; Ford, *The Good Soldier*	Italy joins Allies in war; Gaudier-Brzeska killed in battle
1916	*Lustra* (from which he is forced to remove "indecorous" poems). *Gaudier-Brzeska: A Memoir*. *Noh* translations (from Fenollosa's notes)	Tzara and Arp lead "Dada" movement in Zurich; Lewis, *Tarr* serialized in the *Egoist*; Moore, Stevens, Williams publishing in New York	Battles of Verdun and Ypres; Easter uprising in Dublin; Wilson re-elected; Lloyd George forms war cabinet

1917	"Three Cantos" ("Ur-Cantos") in Poetry, to be much revised before their present form. Eliot's Ezra Pound, His Metric and Poetry. Joyce, in Zurich, sends first chapters of Ulysses.	Eliot, Prufrock and Other Observations; Valéry, La jeune parque; Apollinaire, Les Mamelles de Tirésias; Satie and Picasso collaborate on Parade; Prokofiev, "Classical" Symphony	United States declares war on Germany; in October, American troops in France; Lenin leads successful Bolshevik revolt against Kerensky's government, signs armistice with Germany
1918	Encounters C. H. Douglas and Social Credit; begins study of economics and money in history. Begins friendship with Marianne Moore.	Ulysses begins serial publication; Diaghalev's Russian ballet amazes London; Spengler, The Decline of the West (vol. 1)	Allied victory; Armistice signed November 11
1919	Quia Pauper Amavi, includes Homage to Sextus Propertius. "The Fourth Canto." Writes versions of Cantos 5-7 and 14-15. Publishes Fenollosa's "The Chinese Written Character"	Schwitters, Merz art; Duchamps draws beard and moustache on the Mona Lisa; Brancusi, Bird in Space; Hardy, Collected Poems; Bauhaus founded in Weimar	Treaty of Versailles; Mussolini forms Fascisti dei Combattimente; National Socialist party founded in Germany; Red Army battles White Army in Russia
1920	Hugh Selwyn Mauberley. Leaves London for Paris	Eliot, The Sacred Wood; Williams, Kora in Hell; Colette, Chéri	U.S. Senate rejects League of Nations and Versailles Treaty
1921	Paris contacts include Joyce, Ford, Hemingway, Brancusi, Cocteau. Dadaists. Correspondent for the Dial (NY). Works on manuscripts of Eliot's The Waste Land. Difficulty finding style and form for Cantos	Lawrence, Women in Love; Svevo, The Confessions of Zeno; Pirandello, Six Characters in Search of an Author	War reparations imposed on Germany; first Fascists elected to Italian parliament
1922	"The Eighth Canto" (now Canto 2). Meets the violinist, Olga Rudge	Eliot, The Waste Land; Joyce, Ulysses	Fascist "march on Rome" (October); Mussolini appointed Prime Minister

Year	Pound	Arts and Letters	History
1923	Works on Malatesta cantos (8-11), two of which appear in Eliot's *Criterion*. *Indiscretions* (prose). Composes an opera, *Villon*	Williams, *Spring and All*; Stevens, *Harmonium*; Rilke, *Duino Elegies*; Schoenberg, twelve-tone composition; Cummings, *The Enormous Room*	All non-Fascist parties dissolved in Italy; Primo de Rivera is Spanish dictator
1924	With Dorothy, leaves Paris for Rapallo. Olga Rudge moves to San Ambrogio, nearby	Moore, *Observations*, Breton, *Surrealist Manifesto*; Mann, *The Magic Mountain*	Hitler imprisoned for nine months; non-Fascist trade unions banned in Italy, Lenin dies; Stalin comes to power
1925	*A Draft of XVI Cantos*. Birth of his daughter, Mary, to Olga Rudge	Kafka's *The Trial* published; Woolf, *Mrs Dalloway*; Yeats, *A Vision*; Hemingway, *In Our Time*	
1926	*Personae* (collected shorter poems). Birth of son, Omar, to Dorothy. *Villon* performed at Paris	Berg, *Wozzeck*; MacDiarmid, *A Drunk Man Looks at the Thistle*; Hughes, *The Weary Blues*	General Strike in Britain; Hirohito becomes Emperor of Japan; Mussolini Developing the "Corporate State"
1927	Begins friendship with Zukofsky. Increasing admiration for Mussolini		
1928	*A Draft of the Cantos, 17-27*. First translation from Confucius	Yeats, *The Tower*; Harlem Renaissance (Hughes, Hurston and others)	Parliamentary government abolished in Italy
1930	*A Draft of XXX Cantos* (in Paris)	Eliot, *Ash Wednesday*; Auden, *Poems*, Lewis, *The Apes of God*	World-wide economic collapse
1931	For the next decade increasingly frenetic economic propaganda	Woolf, *The Waves*; Matisse, *The Dance* (Philadelphia)	Republican government in Spain
1933	*ABC of Economics*. Writes *Jefferson and/or Mussolini* (published 1935)	Yeats, *The Winding Stair*; Neruda, *Residence on Earth* (I)	Hitler appointed Chancellor. All non-Nazi political parties banned
1934	*Eleven New Cantos (31-41)*. *ABC of Reading*. *Make it New* (prose)	Stein-Thompson, *Four Saints in Three Acts*	Italy invades Ethiopia; Hitler and Mussolini meet in June
1937	*The Fifth Decad of Cantos (42-51)*	Picasso, *Guernica*	Stalin's purge trials in Moscow

Year			
1938	*Guide to Kulchur*	Sartre, *Nausea*	German troops enter Austria
1939	Brief visit to United States, believing he can help prevent the coming war	Joyce, *Finnegans Wake*; Yeats, *Last Poems*	Germans invade Czechoslovakia, and Poland: World War II begins
1940	*Cantos 52-71*. January: begins semi-crazed broadcasts on Rome Radio	Hemingway, *For Whom the Bell Tolls*; Wright, *Native Son*	Italy declares war on Allies; fall of France; Battle of Britain
1941			Japanese bomb Pearl Harbor, United States enters the war; Italy declares war on USSR
1942	Tries to return to America, but is unable to do so. Radio broadcasts claim he will not say anything "incompatible with his duties as a citizen of the United States"	Eliot, *Little Gidding* (last of the *Four Quartets*); Camus, *The Stranger*	United States at war; fierce fighting in Pacific and Europe; Germans in siege of Leningrad
1943	Indicated for treason by United States. Last radio broadcast in July. Supports Mussolini's Salò Republic	Dylan Thomas, *New Poems*	Allies invade Italy; Mussolini deposed, arrested, rescued by Germans. Italy surrenders Sept. 9
1944	Writes Cantos 72-73 (in Italian)		Mussolini forms 'Salò Republic'
1945	Arrested by American troops. Six months in military prison, where he writes the *Pisan Cantos*, translates Confucius. Flown to Washington, judged unfit to stand trial, remains in St Elizabeths Hospital for the insane to May 1958	Orwell, *Animal Farm*; Auden, *For the Time Being*; Henry Green, *Loving*; Waugh, *Brideshead Revisited*; Calder, *Red Pyramid* (mobile)	Allied victory in Europe, then in Pacific, after U.S. drops atom bomb on Hiroshima; Hitler's suicide; Mussolini executed by partisans
1947	*Confucius: The Unwobbling Pivot and The Great Digest* (translations)	Mann, *Doctor Faustus*; Duncan, *Heavenly City, Earthly City*	
1948	*The Pisan Cantos* (74-84)	Williams, *Paterson* (Book 2)	
1950	*The Letters of Ezra Pound*, ed. D. D. Paige. Confucian *Analects*	Bishop, "Visits to St Elizabeths"	Korean war begins. China invades Tibet

1953	*The Translations of Ezra Pound*, ed. Hugh Kenner	Beckett, *The Unnamable*; Barthes, *Writing Degree Zero*	Death of Stalin; armistice in Korean War
1954	*Literary Essays*, ed. T. S. Eliot. Translation of the Confucian Odes	"Movement" poets active (Larkin, Davie and others)	Algerian uprising against French rule
1955	*Section: Rock-Drill* (Cantos 85-95)	Nabokov, *Lolita*; Lewis, *Self-Condemned*; Baldwin, *Notes of a Native Son*	Warsaw Defense Pact
1956	Sophocles, *Women of Trachis* (translation)	Ginsberg, *Howl*; MacDiarmid, *In Memoriam James Joyce*	Kruschev denounces Stalin; Hungarian revolt suppressed by Soviets
1958	Government dismisses indictment for treason. Released from St Elizabeths, returns to Italy, settling first with daughter, Mary, at Brunnenburg	Beckett, *Krapp's Last Tape*; Williams, *Paterson* (Book 5)	First earth satellites placed in orbit by USSR; European Economic Community founded; Lebanon requests aid of U.S. troops
1959	*Thrones* (Cantos 96-109), written mostly at Washington. From late 1959 on he finds it hard to concentrate, and is able to write little	Snyder, *Riprap*; Rexroth, *Bird in the Bush*; "Pop Art" movement	Castro takes power in Cuba; Dalai Lama forced to flee Tibet
1961	Estranged from Dorothy, lives with Olga at San Ambrogio and Venice. Increasing depression and sense of failure. Falls into silence, speaking rarely in his final years	Ginsberg, *Kaddish*; Cage, *Silence*; Beckett, *How it is*, *Happy Days*; Thom Gunn, *My Sad Captains*	Yuri Gagarin is first man in space; East Germans erect Berlin Wall; crisis over Soviet missiles in Cuba
1969	*Drafts and Fragments of Cantos* (110-117). Mostly written earlier	Tarn, *The Beautiful Contradictions*	First men on moon
1972	Dies at Venice, 1 November		Nixon opens relations with China

Chapter 1

Towards reading the Cantos

Magnanimity / magnanimity /
   I know I ask a great deal
                         unpublished draft of Canto 84

By 1926, James Joyce and his friend, admirer and most vigorous publicist, Ezra Pound, were launched on the two long, difficult works which were to be their last – *Finnegans Wake* and the *Cantos*. From Paris, "Jim the comedian" (74/433) sent Pound, now settled in Rapallo, an early version of the *Wake*, but Ez, for all his legendary loyalty to old friends, would have none of it. "Dear Jim," he wrote back, "I will have another go at it, but up to present I make nothing of it whatever. Nothing so far as I make out, nothing short of divine vision or a new cure for the clapp can possibly be worth all the circumambient peripherization" (*L* 202). There is more here than the comedy of leading *avant-gardistes* unable to deal with each other's most extreme texts (Joyce showed even less interest in the *Cantos*). The sub-text of Pound's snappy critique was precisely that his own ambitious poem did contain, or aspired to, both divine vision *and* cures for social disease – that is, for war, poverty, hunger, misgovernment and institutionalized oppression. Morever, the "long poem containing history" was based on a profound intuition that vision and cure were interdependent. Like Dante's *Divine Comedy*, the poem with which this most intertextual of texts is closely interwoven, the *Cantos*, while it wishes always to be *divertente* [entertaining] (41/202), is distinctly a didactic poem. It invites us to accompany its pilgrim/poet on a difficult, non-linear journey out of darkness towards light, in the course of which we meet innumerable examples of the blessed and the damned, as well as of every gradation between. In the course of that journey, we hear many specific judgements and interpretations of history, some of which are at best idiosyncratic, at worst bizarre or rebarbative. Of greater importance than those judgements, some of which we will agree with, some not, is the poet's invitation to join him in an active "volitionist" state of mind, a lively and holistic "awareness" leading toward "directio voluntatis [*direction of the will*], as lord over the heart" (77/467). The poem urges us away from despair ("the wrong way about it" [89/598]), passivity, conformity, selfishness and received ideas and language ("Make it new!"), and towards such virtues as responsibility, an active sensibility and benevolence. We are told, through the voice/text of the fifth-century BC Pythagorean philosopher Ocellus, that it is "our job to build light" (98/684).

Pleasing, teaching, moving

The *Cantos* constantly supplies hints about its own poetics. None is more important than the trinity Pound borrows from medieval rhetoric, quoted in whole or in fragments several times, *ut moveat, ut doceat, ut delectat*, that it move, teach and delight. At given moments one may come to the fore, casting the others for a while in shadow, but at its greatest, its most intense, poetry brings all three within equal balance or tension. Pound never abandons his desire for the aesthetic, in the sense of the pleasurable, the beautiful, yet by the time the poem as we now have it began to take shape (about 1917), he had turned his back on aesthetic*ism*. "My aesthetic period may in the long run look like an interlude" (*CC* 321). It would be fruitless to posit an exact date for the end of that interlude, which presumably embraced most of the work gathered in *Personae* and *Collected Early Poems*. Two events contributed to the move away from aestheticism toward a direct engagement with contemporary social problems. The first was the slaughter of the First World War, treated directly, stripped of any trace of romance, in Canto 16. The war brought a personal loss for which Pound never ceased to grieve: the death in the trenches in 1915 of his companion in the avant-garde Vorticist movement, the young sculptor, Henri Gaudier-Brzeska. Years later he wrote:

For eighteen years the death of Henri Gaudier has been unremedied ... With a hundred fat rich men working overtime to start another war or another six wars for the sake of their personal profit, it is very hard for me to write of Gaudier with the lavender tones of dispassionate reminiscence. (*GB* 140)

He thought 1918 the year he "began investigation of causes of war, to oppose same." Things fell decisively into place in 1919, when he encountered the economic theories of C. H. Douglas, "directed toward a more humane standard of life; directed to the prevention of new wars" (*SP* 212:*182*). From that time on, the *Cantos*, too, would be so directed. It would be a poem containing history and working within history, with the all-important qualification (here Pound is parodying the notorious dictum of Henry Ford) that "History that omits economics is mere bunk" (*GK* 259).

The sequence *Hugh Selwyn Mauberley* (1920), the last substantial poem Pound wrote before devoting himself exclusively to the *Cantos*, was a farewell to London and just as distinctly a public farewell to aestheticism. The word "usury" appeared for the first time in his verse, and the career of the poem's anti-hero, Mauberley, registered the impotence of aestheticism when perceptions of beauty remain without application "to relation of the state / To the individual," in an "Irresponse to human aggression." Of course, the concept of didactic art required redefinition, for didactic verse appeared to run counter to hard-won premises of literary modernism, in particular that art should not point a moral or tell the reader directly what to think. In inventing the "Imagist"movement (1912–13) Pound had warned poets, "Don't be 'viewy' – leave that to the writers of pretty little philosophic essays" (*LE* 6). He had, then, to propose for the *Cantos* a "profounder didacticism," distinct from art as "patent medicine," a profounder *ut doceat* working through "revelation" (*L* 180).

There will always be readers who resist a text with moral and political designs upon them, and grand designs at that.

Others, less resisting, may yet feel themselves too often beyond the *Cantos*' magnetic field, its intricate weaving, maze or arcanum (a few of the many metaphors the poem uses for itself). Such readers are unlikely to find the poem attractive enough to justify the alert study and attention it invites. Many will be content to read selectively, enjoying resonant or curious single lines or short units, without much regard for their often bewildering contexts:

> night green of his pupil, as grape flesh and sea wave
> (74/432)

> Under white clouds, cielo di Pisa,
> out of all this beauty something must come,

> O moon my pin-up . . .   (84/539)

There are attractive, more extended lyrical passages, such as the famous Canto 13, Confucius walking by a dynastic temple; Canto 45, the great denunciatory chant against Usura; the Ovidian Canto 2, a ship turning to stone, panthers formed from air, men turning to fish; the Ignez de Castro passage, beginning "Time is the evil" (30/147–48); or lines that require of the reader nothing other than sensitivity to the rapid movement of emotion:

> and to know beauty and death and despair
> and to think what has been shall be,
> flowing, ever unstill.

> Then a partridge-shaped cloud over dust storm.
> The hells move in cycles,
> No man can see his own end.
> The Gods have not returned. "They have never left us."
> They have not returned.
> Cloud's processional and the air moves with their living.
> (113/787)

Readers are particularly attracted, as well, to the moving "confessional" passage of the Pisan cantos and *Drafts and Fragments*, where the poet abandons masks, personae and texts to consider his errors and failures of charity, his imprisonment, or his dark night of the soul, when "the loneliness of death came upon me / (at 3 P.M., for an instant)'' (82/527). Yet clearly the more readily appealing lyrical, autobiographical or comprehensible passages are one thing, the *Cantos* another. Beauty, limpidity, meaning, if they are not to be sentimental or specious, nor serve, Pound thought, as an ideological soporific pleasing to the masters of our ''hell of mercantilist industrialism'' (*GK* 167), are achieved only after considerable effort, research and learning on the part of both poet and reader.

Pound once described the poem as a ''record of struggle,'' noting immediately his awareness of defects inherent in such art, among them that of being ''too interesting'' (*GK* 135). ''Beauty is difficult,'' runs as a motif throughout the Pisan cantos, as Pound quotes Aubrey Beardsley speaking to Yeats, who had asked why he drew horrors. ''So very difficult, Yeats, beauty so difficult'' (80/511). And when, toward the end of his life, Pound made a *Selected Cantos*, as introduction to the ''whole poem,'' he refused, rather doughtily, an easy appeal to readers by privileging the ''caressible'' at the expense of pages representative of the poem at its most difficult. Whatever pleasures or illuminations we derive from the poem will presumably be more authentic, more truly our own, to the extent that we have won through to them. It is a strange aesthetic, perhaps, that bars us from so many familiar points of entry into art, but we may take courage in the characteristically optimistic Poundian thought that ''If a man starts noticing ANYthing, there is no telling what he mayn't notice next'' (*GK* 282).

It would be wrong, if understandable, for the new reader/ starer-at-these-pages to assume that the *Cantos* has, or ever had, a ready audience, some pre-existent élite, to which he/she does not potentially belong. It is, after all, a poem which in large part the poet himself could never have read until he had written it: Pound, like the rest of us, used cribs and bilingual editions; many of the events the poem records, both public and private, had not yet happened as he began to write; nor had most of the documents and philosophical and literary works it weaves into its expansive, disseminative ex-ploration yet been discovered by the weaver. The Pound of

1925, when the first sixteen cantos appeared in a severely limited edition, after about a decade of experiments and false starts, or the poet of the 1930 *A Draft of XXX Cantos*, knew nothing, or next to nothing, about materials that were to enter the poem in succeeding instalments through 1969. Pound might reasonably expect the reader to have a sense of Homer and Dante and some familiarity with Greek myth, but these do not take us far along the path. There was no pre-existent audience for the poem, neither for its content nor for its ways of proceeding. In no text do reading and writing more closely approximate each other, and Pound continually dramatizes his *acts* of reading and interpretation, which do not really precede the writing. Moreover, he knows (much of the time) what he is doing and what difficulties we may be having. "I shall have to learn a little greek to keep up with this," he growled from the page in 1956, "but so will you, drratt you" (105/750).

No Aquinas map

The poet often points to differences between his poem and its greatest analogue, the *Divine Comedy*. In somewhat defensive replies to sympathetic, yet complaining readers he argued that Dante's orderly cosmology – Hell, Purgatory, Heaven, each with gradations of circles or planetary spheres – was no longer available to the modern poet (*L* 190, 293). Dante's poem is in fact not all that orderly or sorted out – "paradisal" elements occur in its hell, "infernal" elements in its paradise; yet in an obvious sense, when you are reading Dante you know where you are, and in Pound often you don't. Pound, and by implication the modern world, with its anarchy of competing world-views and values, had available no "Aquinas-map; Aquinas *not* valid now" (*L* 323). "Map" here signifies not only imaginative poetic geography, albeit of "states, not places" (*SR* 128), but anything resembling the ordered conceptual–moral scheme found in the writings of St Thomas. In the twentieth century a *Summa* is not attainable. However, more important for Pound than the disappearance of divine geography, with its possibilities for poetic form, is the withdrawal of the Logos, in the sense of a commonly agreed upon or authorizing Truth for the poem. The young Pound, already aware of the difficulties before him, believed that Dante "*sought* to hang his song from the absolute" (my emphasis: note the trace of doubt). That absolute had vanished, or become something like Bradley's Absolute, a word to solve philosophers' problems, at best an invention to satisfy the nostalgic space created by the Death of God and the shutdown of mysticism (so Pound's friend, Eliot, had decided, in his Harvard dissertation). Art, after Dante's time, "has for the most part built from the ground" (*SR* 166). In an age when there are no givens − except perhaps a dominant ideology which Pound insists it is incumbent upon us to shatter by acts of perception (*GK* 281–83) − we find ourselves bewildered among interpretations of texts already much-interpreted. We are each of us left, as Wallace Stevens said, to put the world together, but not with our hands. Everything must be looked at and considered as if never seen before. "Begin where you are" (52/261) Pound tells us, which, for a serious poet of his generation, meant beginning where Dante did not have to begin, at thought degree zero.

For the reader of the *Cantos* something else available to Dante is missing, something yet more important to our practical problems as readers − a dependable guide. Dante's pilgrim, as we travel with him, has always at this side some one to answer his questions, to tell him where he is and what he witnesses, to instruct him in history and theology as needed − Virgil, Beatrice, Bernard of Clairvaux. And even if we say we have lost faith that such guides, or the phantom "reliable narrator," are capable of telling us the whole story about any text, we still find their presence reassuring. In the *Cantos*, as in so many modernist works − *Ulysses*, *The Waste Land*, *Four Saints in Three Acts* − even as the text proffers hints for interpretation, the reader may well bear greater responsibilities than he or she feels ready to cope with. I will suggest, below, an initial way of coping (briefly: relax and pay attention). Yet we should note that the absence of a

Virgilian guide within the *Cantos* is momentous: an absence whose presence is always with us. We must remember, however, that one of the richer complexities of the poem is that Pound acts both as pilgrim and guide. He is the explorer capable of doubts and of a sophisticated sense of the problems of interpretation, and the hurler of judgemental bolts; and *neither ever completely subsumes the other*. Pound's "ideogrammic method" — that is, juxtaposition upon juxtaposition combined with extreme compression — often escapes the poet's intention and invites alternate interpretations. And yet . . . one can become fond of these brooding undecidables. To insist too much upon coherence, clarity and consistency would be to demand a *Cantos* without its unique concentrations and seductions.

Reading Canto 31

The greatest impediment to reading the *Cantos* is a demand to know too much, too soon. Pound at times posited a reader who would principally attend to "what is *on the page*" (*L* 321). In 1954, on the dust jacket of a Faber edition, he wished for a critic who would "read through them before stopping to wonder whether he or she is understanding them: I think he or she will find at the end that he or she has." This is excellent (if optimistic) advice, which few have sufficient patience, courage or suspension of disbelief to follow. But let us look, as if with an innocent eye, at Canto 31, the beginning of the sequence Pound came to call "Jefferson — Nuevo Mundo," the first extended treatment of American history in the poem. It is useful for our purpose because it is short and almost entirely written in/quoted from English, thus relieving us for the time being of an impulse to reach for Greek or Chinese dictionaries. But what is trivial here and what becomes important? What, if we don't stop to "understand," might we find we have understood after all?

Reading the first thirty cantos, we will have become aware that (even apart from tags in "foreign" languages) the poem is not written in English, but in a variety of Englishes, each bringing with it at least some tone or coloration. We have already heard, among other tones and voices, the archaic, the lyrical, the flat and the sublime, the peaceful and violent, and modern American dialects, as well as a number of highly artificial versions of English representing Confucian China, the Italian Renaissance in both its civilizing and its savage aspects, and so forth. All pasts and all languages of which we have record can be drawn to this writing, this present-in-motion. Here in Canto 31, we appear to encounter an English new to the poem, the eighteenth-century American of, mostly, Thomas Jefferson: in part as suggesting its time (note how often "time" is specified), in part as registering qualities of mind that were Jefferson's. It is in fact not an entirely new English: as we begin Canto 31, there may at least linger in memory a page containing a letter of Jefferson's ten cantos earlier (21/97). At that point we had no reason to suspect that either Jefferson (and with him much that he comes to stand for) or "American history" were to become major elements in the poem. In Canto 21, however, there may have been imprinted in our minds traces of Jefferson's wide-ranging interests, in particular his "civilizing" concern for crafts and art (even if we wondered *why Jefferson*?).

By the time we had reached that page in Canto 21, we could not have escaped noticing that meaning in the *Cantos* is often produced by contrast and abrupt shifts in focus. If we are sensitive to Pound's unexplained contrasts, we observe that Jefferson's letter in Canto 21 stands in tone and content as a small "paradisal" island of language surrounded by talk of war, murder, assassination, bribery, chicanery, grotesque personal luxury ("a gold collar holding a diamond / That cost about 3000 ducats") and the mentality of private gain without concern for public good ("Keep on with the business, / That's made me, / And the res publica didn't"). Yet as we first encounter it in Canto 21, we have no way of knowing that "Jefferson" is to be heard as a musical leading tone or motif later to be developed at length.

When that leading tone reappears in Canto 31, it soon includes Jefferson's friend, fellow revolutionary and nation-builder, John Adams, with whom the reader will eventually develop a more extended and affectionate familiarity; it then moves rapidly forward in history, with compare-and-contrast interruptions to Canto 37, into the administrations of Jackson and Van Buren, as Pound constructs a line of investigation of American political economy with which we will not concern ourselves here (briefly: public control of the nation's money and credit). Yet in Canto 31 we are faced, as always in Pound, with not knowing, if the text has not established them for us, the relative weights of names and phrases. Patience is required. The first thirty cantos should have prepared us, too, for Pound's technique of "subject-rhyme" and the fact that there are recurrences in history: Jefferson's concern for opening up communications, building a canal and improving navigation rhyme with a number of things, among them Confucius's "Get up and do something useful" (13/59), and with such valuable civic acts as Palmerston's draining swamps and dredging a harbor in Sligo (52/261). All these stand in contrast to innumerable destructive or obstructive acts, and to the lotus-eating voices that moan, "Nothing I build / And I reap / Nothing" (27/132).

Or take the repeated "no slaves": this leads backwards and forwards to at least twenty-four condemnations of slavery, usually literal, sometimes figurative, beginning with the sailors "Mad for a little slave money," who attempt to kidnap the young god, Bacchus–Dionysus, in Canto 2, and continuing with the praise of Cunizza da Romano, who "freed her slaves on a Wednesday" (6/22). We may or may not know Cunizza as the lover of the troubador. Sordello, and as a joyous light in the third heaven – that of Venus – in Dante's *Paradiso*. We do not need to know who she was in order to recall, when we meet her in later cantos, that she is a figure of charity and love; nor to see, again by conscious or unconscious recall, that she and Jefferson are brought within a field of attraction by "no slaves." Likewise, we have no need to know what in particular made Jefferson complain of "English papers . . . their lies." The concept of falsified reports and bought media is established, and echoes back to the clattering presses, press-gang and hired liars of the usurers' Hell of Canto 14, forward to an attack on the BBC (76/458) and to many passages opening outward from the concept of "forging false news" (67/398).

What is most important about Canto 31 is its tonality, the flavour of Jefferson's and Adams's precise and inquisitive minds, the sounds of their prose and whatever those sounds bring along (including, rather conspicuously, comments on the burdens of high taxation and interest payments). Another day, we may feel it necessary or interesting to know what lies "behind" these snippets. That is not hard to find out: scholars have done the work for us. Yet with all contexts and fuller versions of the documents before us, there remains the challenge of reading the canto as a poem which is part of a larger poem. We may well find that research, having all the "history" spelled out for us, is as much an obstruction as a help toward that goal, a distraction from the pleasures of the text. What are we to make of the parenthetical "*parts of this letter in cypher*"? These are, by the way, the only words in this canto "written" by Pound, and yet he has written over and under all the other words, which had their previous incarnations in the writings of Adams, Madison and Jefferson. Is the remark about cipher a self-reflexive joke, that is, for *cypher* should we read *canto*? I have argued at length elsewhere that we have in a sense two poems here, written in identical words, one largely of surface, the other with a deeper structure, a modern turn on the troubador *trobar clus* or "hidden style"; that the deeper structure is fully revealed only when we leave the poem, turn to the documents, and see what Pound has left out; and that the deeper significance is perhaps more than the cryptic surface can reasonably be expected to lead us towards (Kearns 81–86).

To what extent my reading/deciphering of that hidden poem is just or merely over-ingenious, is not the point. I learned a great deal as I enjoyed inventing and/or revealing it; my experience, for what it is worth, is that Pound has seldom brought me into a corner of the library which was not interesting – and some of the corners have been odd indeed.

There is nothing odd, however, about the Adams-Jefferson correspondence, however, one of the unread splendours of American literature. The questions, of course, are those we have with any highly allusive text, as in *The Waste Land* and *Ulysses*, and are exacerbated in the *Cantos*: where does one stop? Must one stop? Absolutely? Provisionally? A key term in Pound's poetics is *logopoeia*, the "dance of intellect" among "the concomitant meanings, customs, usages, and implied contexts of the words themselves" — the dance which forms a trinity with *phanopoeia*, images for the visual imagination, and *melopoeia*, sound, which in perhaps mysterious but perceptible ways places a charge upon meaning (*SP* 321). That dance, for Pound, is among words as they live in written or spoken language, yet logopoeia clearly implies, also, the dance of intellect among texts. "Ply over ply," the *Cantos* says of itself, at least six times, beginning at 4/15. Play over play. Ply/play suggests a "give" in the fabric of reading, but how much? Joyce cancelled the question with his *Wake* — as did Gertrude Stein, differently, in *Tender Buttons* — by inviting us to supplement the text into infinity with any plays on words he (inadvertently?) may have overlooked. We have seen that Pound refused to undertake that journey, finding Joyce's post-*Ulysses* method (as he found Stein's writing, as well) a "diarrhoea of consciousness" (*L* 292). As always with Pound, we have an enriching conflict of impulses. Gestures towards an infinite opening into textuality, the undecidable, the free association (via play, puns, fanciful etymologies, fortuitous homophones, superimposition of images, texts and languages) is balanced by an unwavering longing for "the total sincerity, the precise definition" (77/468). "Precise terminology is the first implement" (99/7111) and, through the voice of Ford Madox Ford, we are instructed to get "A DICtionary / and learn the meaning of words!" (98/689; 100/719). Pound's work with, and extensions of, dictionaries is often quite creative, in the sense of "creative accounting." Yet he will deconstruct his and others' texts only up to a point.

Not yet demanding to know everything possible about

Canto 31 — what *is* Gosindi's Syntagma, what *was* the state of things in 1785, what did Adams think about the church of St Peter, and so forth — attempting to read it as a complex of impressions, with echoes and overtones from earlier cantos and with the potential for development in later ones, we may have understood, or at least noticed, a good deal. We have listened to the tonality of Jefferson's and Adam's minds and language, and considered the possibility that political leaders may have a wide-ranging curiosity and culture; in contrast to the intelligence of these speakers, we hear of ignorance in high places. Among the themes touched upon are the complexities of human nature and motives; the evils of slavery, taxation and interest payments; and the opening of canals/channels of communication. There is a resistance to the abstract and general, to an insensitive and impractical rigidity of ideology, by way of specifying conditions and actions at certain times. Error, once begun, is hard to contain. While one may believe in human reason and conscience (Adams's faith in them is prefaced by an ominous "though"), "Man" is not wholly rational, but is subject to "kinks" and appetites. Although there is doubt about the dignity and benevolence of "human nature," we may hope, at least, for a return "to sentiments / worthy of former times." More important than any concept, any bit of history, is the canto's registration of active men with intelligent and benevolent minds struggling, as are presumably poet and reader, through an opposition marked by error, ignorance and some more dubious aspects of human nature. To that extent, Canto 31 is a model for the central poetic and ethical intelligence within the *Cantos*, which is suggested by the last line of the poem, "To be men not destroyers."

Yet clearly, reading for "what is on the page" leaves us with unanswered questions about this canto. Only "research" of one sort or another will begin to answer them. For example: the Latin motto with which the canto begins, "Tempus loquendi, / Tempus tacendi," translates Ecclesiastes, "A time to speak, a time to be silent." One can trace themes of speaking and silence, both for good and for ill, within the canto. Yet nowhere does the *Cantos* give us a clue (in what ways does it matter?) that Sigismundo Malatesta, an important figure in the poem and the principal subject of Cantos 8–11, inscribed the words *tempus tacendi, tempus loquendi* on the tomb of his beloved Isotta, within his half-pagan Renaissance temple, a monument to his ego and to his devotion to classical culture ("There is no other single man's effort equally registered" [*GK*, frontispiece]).

> Take away appetite, and the present generation would not
> Live a month, and no future generation would exist;
> and thus the exalted dignity of human nature etc. ....
>   Mr Adams to Mr Jefferson, 15 Nov. 1813.
> "..wish that I cd. subjoin Gosindi's Syntagma
> "of the doctrines of Epicurus.
>   (Mr Adams.)
> "this was the state of things in 1785..."
>   (Mr Jefferson.)

Do we feel we can't go on without knowing more about Adams's thoughts on Gosindi and Epicurus? Research informs us that the remark wasn't made by Adams after all – the typography, or Pound's mistake, misleads. It's from a letter of Jefferson's, in which he finds the doctrine of Epicurus "the most rational system remaining of the philosophy of the ancients." Rather disappointing, but at least we can more firmly read Pound's snippet as indicating – what? His or Jefferson's approval of Epicurus? Their interest in the classics?

Adams, in a letter to Jefferson of 2 February 1816, thought St Peter's in Rome a "stupendous Monument of human Hypocricy and Fanaticism." As we read on in that letter, we discover that what Pound has included may be less illuminating than what he has left out: "human Reason and human Conscience, though I believe there are such things, are not a Match, for human Passions, human Imaginations and human Enthusiasm." There is no way to decide with certainty the meaning of the omission.

Do we feel we've missed the point of the remark about Holy Scripture?

A tiel leis . . . en ancien scripture, and this
they have translated *Holy Scripture* . . .
                                    Mr Jefferson
and they continue this error.

In a letter to Adams of 1814, Jefferson quotes a fifteenth-
century legal opinion that "to such laws [*a tiel leis*] of the
church as have warrent in ancient writing [*en ancien
scripture*] our law giveth credence." An early falsification by
mistranslation turned this into "such laws of the church as
have warrent in *holy scripture*," and the error was continued
in law for centuries. Jefferson concludes with the dry comment, "who can question but that the whole Bible and Testament are part of the Common Law?" Interesting, and with
that knowledge we can make all sorts of thematic connections
to concerns of the *Cantos* (for example, falsifications of
language and Coke's great work on the Common Law,
celebrated in Cantos 107–109). By now, however, we are a
considerable distance from "what is *on the page*."

Usurious reading

To spend even a short time with the *Cantos* is to become
aware of the inadequacy of "reading," that word we use to
indicate so many and such varied activities. What does it
mean to read such a text, which asks us to perform extraordinary feats of memory, interpretation and study; which
refuses to help us with coherent narrative or clear structure or
guidelines; which often seems to be driving us away from
itself and towards Pound's prose, Professor Terrell's invaluable *Companion*, a shelf of criticism growing faster than
it can be assimilated, and all the writings, architecture, paintings, and music Pound has built into his new construction?
Familiarity with the poem and its materials will develop in
patches, not sequentially page after page. Interpretations open
into each other, requiring us to read backwards as well as forwards. Each reader will make different decisions about which
sections he or she chooses to "work on," and in what order
– or by what predilection or accident – materials come to

hand. Resonances accumulate over time. Readings take place in three dimensions, with the reward, perhaps, of an occasional glimpse into "The fourth; the dimension of stillness" (49/245). In short, the true reader of the *Cantos* must take pleasure in suspension of meaning rather than closure.

Moreover, the very ethic of the poem suggests, requires, an ethic of reading: both in the writing and in our cumulative knowledge and interpretation, the *Cantos* is a communal project. On every page, the poet implicitly or explicitly inveighs against possessiveness and the *"grab-at-once* state of mind" (*GK* 41). He identifies himself four times as "ego, scriptor" [I, the writer], *scriptor* implying "transcriber," the one who happens now to be working on "this palimpsest" (116/797), more than "author" in the sense of owner of the experience, of unique, inspired or authorizing source. (When Pound uses "author" of himself, it is always with an ironic glance at the word's pretensions.) So the text informs us, not as Ezra Pound speaking alone, but through the voice of an ancient Chinese "scriptor," himself writing through a series of other texts:

> This is not a work of fiction
> 　　　　　nor yet of one man:　　　　　(99/708)

Pound could not be more clear about this, writing here in the prose *Guide to Kulchur*, but with words equally valid for the poem:

There is no ownership to my statements and I cannot interrupt every sentence or paragraph to attribute authorships [note the plural] to each pair of words, especially as there is seldom an a priori claim even to the phrase or half-phase.　　　　　(*GK* 60)

All of which suggests an ethic of reading a text which has so many gaps and crossings of codes that we can neither be enclosed by it nor hope to "master" it. That is, we must read without avarice. There will never be a final understanding to be deposited in our account at the Bank of Culture. We can only posit a series of readings different in time and in kind. In the course of those readings we find ourselves performing some activities we associate with reading and many we do not, such as: staring at, guessing at, performing music (Canto 75 and the opening of 91); decoding Egyptian hieroglyphics; seeing the running legs of a horse within a Chinese ideogram; learning to recognize odd little drawings as signs of temples and mountains; and flipping pages backwards and forwards. One way or another, we are inevitably drawing up the index Marianne Moore dryly thought Pound should have supplied with the poem. Some readings may produce, literally, more writing than reading: in the first copy of the *Cantos* I owned there are pages with more words written in the white spaces by me than were placed there by the printer.

Reading *from* Canto 92

In the 1930s his friend Wyndham Lewis called Pound a man in love with the past, and variations on that accusation have continued. Is the *Cantos* an exercise in nostalgia or not? I think it a wrong-headed reading to find Pound seriously romanticizing or wanting to return to any past; the spirit of his rummaging in history and ancient texts is that of "not regarding the past as something to be seen in mere retrospect but as key to parts of the future" (*CC* 329). If not nostalgic, however, Pound's history is usually idiosyncratic, at times quite unreliable: he will believe anything he reads if it suits his purpose. Selected, highly interpreted figures and works of art arise before us as examples of wisdom, vision, beauty or civic virtue − arise often suddenly from surrounding confusion or evil, only to vanish or to be obscured. A powerful image of the tragedy of history comes at 16/69 where, on a Dantesque journey out of hell toward a classical Elysium, we pass a repulsive lake of dead water swarming with a confusion of bodies, limbs and embryos, like fish "heaped in a bin." In the midst of that lake there appears an "arm upward, clutching a fragment of marble" − only to be "submerged by the eels." The image is of the poem itself, particularly the first thirty cantos, in which moments of beauty or achievement are glimpsed amidst an often indecipherable, messy, blood-and-treachery version of the Italian Renaissance. A movement, which we may figure roughly as dark/light/dark, or hell/ paradise/hell, is one of the large-scale rhythms of the *Cantos*.

That rhythm, with its accompanying emotions, can be felt in the concluding lines of Canto 92, a passage that is as much a meditation on history as are those sections of the poem reserved for digests of the histories of China and the United States. We observe a number of pasts being drawn into an active present:

> And against usury
>> and the degradation of sacraments,
> For 40 years I have seen this,
>> now flood as the Yang tse
> also desensitization
>> 25 hundred years desensitization
>> 2 thousand years, desensitization
> After Apollonius, desensitization
>> & a little light from the borders:
>> Erigena,
>> Avicenna, Richardus.
> Hilary looked at an oak leaf
>> or holly, or rowan
> as against the brown òil and corpse sweat
> & then cannon to take the chinks opium
> & the Portagoose uprooting spice-trees "a common"
>> sez Ari "custom in trade"

By the time we arrive at these lines we should be familiar with the materials of which they are a lively recombination. (Note, incidentally, the sign of writing, "&," which is also a sign of speed: the eye may take it in a fraction of a blink faster than "and," which the typist/scriptor has no time always to spell out, as he hasn't time to put in all those commas which would slow things down and resist the fusion, as well as the speed, of thought.) The only thing really new to the poem here is the name "Avicenna," the eleventh-century Arabic philosopher-theologian, whom Pound thought the apex of Arab philosophy and a manifestation of spiritual elevation (*SP* 68). In fact Avicenna has been secretly present all along, in the sense that his thought was a living influence within the minds of Dante and Dante's friend Guido Cavalcanti, whose *Donna mi prega*, a canzone on the relation between knowledge and love, is translated mysteriously and beautifully in Canto 36. We should not have to know much about Avicenna, however, to get the point, for we find him here in a trinity with Scotus Erigena and Richard of St Victor, with whom we are presumably familiar from earlier cantos. Three pages on, he reappears in an even more paradisal setting (93/625).

The passage begins in darkness, with *usury*, which has been exemplified and denounced in hundreds of instances. Usury is more than a technical problem of interest rates, standing in the way of adequate housing and food, restricting production of everything good, promoting production of things we do not need for living, notably armaments. By this time *usury* has already been established at length in Cantos 45 and 51 as a state of mind and as the poem's chief sign of evil. It is associated with degradation of the holy (including art and sexuality) and with desensitization: the usurer does not want the rest of us to be quick, informed or aware. The poet, writing these lines in a madhouse in Washington DC in the 1950s, has been observing and fighting usury and its attendant evils since his youth: these lines are one more skirmish in the battle. At the moment the degradation/desensitization appear to be worsening, rising to flood-tide like China's Yellow River. Suddenly, "against" the evil there arise signs of light and nature, associated with names of people whose minds reflect fragments of spiritual–intellectual, anti-usurious light. We have met them before and will meet them again: Apollonius, first-century Pythagorean mystic, seer and wandering guru, is associated with images of clarity, crystal, light, "peace with the animals" (93/623) and "charitas insuperabilis" (invincible love). Scotus Erigena was a medieval neo-platonic philosopher and transmitter of Greek Culture, who saw divine light shining through all things, whose work was condemned as pantheist, and who was – here we are into Poundian history, for there's no real evidence to support it – "probably murdered" (105/751). Richard of St Victor, twelfth-century mystic and theologian, shines in Dante's

Paradiso and is particularly treasured by Pound for the distinctions he draws between cogitation, meditation, and contemplation. "In the first," Pound comments, "the mind flits aimlessly about the object, in the second it circles about it in a methodical manner, in the third it is unified with the object" (*GK* 77). The final state, *cogitatio*, is associated at 87/576 with justice and direction of the will. St Hilary was a fourth-century theologian who observed intelligence in nature, and who, although he "stumbles," like the poet unable to maintain the vision, knows that "the Divine Mind is abundant" (92/620). This is Pound's late mosaic technique. If we follow these names through all their reverberating associations in the poem, we find ourselves in the considerable company of those who in various ways "built light."

Then that light closes down, and we are back in the darkness these figures stand "against," which is now usury-as-imperialism. The British, not averse to profiting from drug traffic, move into China. The Portuguese in Goa create artificial shortages and ensure their monopoly on trade by uprooting spice-trees. But monopoly, as has been known since the time of Ari[stotle], with whom we seem to be on familiar terms, is a common practice in business. As is so often the case, a clearer exposition of what Ari has to do with all this is found in Pound's prose (*SP* 172). The tone of these final lines of Canto 92 is dry, a bit weary perhaps, for this has been a long battle and the flood is rising; the light here is small, coming from the borders/margins of a dominant Usura. Yet the spirit of the poem is buoyant, for all the ill it knows, and as we move into the next canto we find ourselves in a more cheerful and dazzling paradise, which will in turn be interrupted by darkness and usury, as the rhythm continues.

Past and present

Pound is looking for patterns in history and for "luminous details" that can be interpreted for practical purposes, one of which is to establish a scale of values, to act on behalf of a Good larger than his own, as he finds himself, to quote Eliot on *Ulysses*, within "the immense panorama of futility and anarchy which is contemporary history." (Pound would not insist on "contemporary.") From what comes to hand, he knocks together by the most open and (to me) endearing *bricolage*, a mapping he can live with. He hopes his readers will find that map valid, not necessarily in verifiable truth or in accuracy of detail, but in a large-scale pattern of truth. One might venture: a pattern of truth represented. This seems perfectly in line with one of the dominant traditions of Pound's formative years, American pragmatism out of Peirce and William James. My dictionary defines "pragmatics" as "the branch of semiotic dealing with the relationship of signs and symbols to their users," which very neatly points the reader in a direction for reading Pound: the emphasis is on use-value, not on verification. Such an approach to history and the texts history has left behind dissolves chronology and, in any case, one chronology is achieved by excluding a series of others. So for Pound: "We do NOT know the past in chronological sequence. It may be convenient to lay it out anesthetized on the table with dates pasted on here and there, but what we know we know by ripples and spirals eddying out from us and from our own time" (*GK* 60).

We have always the danger, then, of reading something other than the poem by our habitual desire to place in "order" what Pound has so deliberately shuffled. In Cantos 8–11, which concentrate on the career of the fifteenth-century *condottiere* and patron of the arts, Malatesta, we do not only begin in the middle of things but we are always in the middle of things. Pound had at his side reference books that would easily have allowed a chronological life-and-letters together with explanations of Malatesta's ever-shifting political allegiances. What we have, however, is much more affecting if we read it as part of a "poem containing history," not as history dressed up in poetry. The Malatesta cantos, and others in the first thirty, present an impression of the purgatorial confusion, treachery, and sheer moral-political mess of Renaissance Italy. Against that confusion, like that arm holding up its fragment of marble in Canto 16, we discern moments of civilization, construction and benevolence. Yet history in the *Cantos* is distinctly the darkling plain of Matthew Arnold's "Dover Beach." Pound, it should be clear, refuses to settle for the despair of Arnold's seaside vacationer: against the rubble of the past, within its documents so hard to interpret, he finds spots of joy, love, light, some peace (if hard to maintain) and a good deal of help for pain. We are meant to "learn" from Pound's history that there is much for us to do today.

If history in the *Cantos* is to be sorted out at all, it will not be as chronology, certainly not as a demonstration of progress. It is the "Purgatory of human error" (*SP* 167:*137*), much of it a tale of "savages against maniacs / and vice versa" (105/751) — here the poem is in the midst of a cryptic digest of William of Malmesbury's *History of the Kings of England*. Pound's eccentric editing of chronicles has the virtue of stimulating curiosity. It has, at times, the defect of militating against the kind of reading I urge — that is, accepting the poem as it comes.

The *Cantos* is a poem of fragments, it frequently takes the trouble to point out, as if we needed be told. Perhaps it wants us to know that *it* knows. Even as it invites us to make thousands of connections, it reminds us not to destroy its fragmentary character, which is both the source of its particular textual pleasure and a representation of the ways knowledge and experience come to us. Pound criticism, more than most criticism, is self-defeating — pages of often ingeniously researched and interpreted backgrounds and sources take us farther and farther from the poem. To the tangle of activities we call reading the *Cantos*, then, we must add forgetting everything except what it has become impossible to forget because either the poem or its marginalia have left traces in the mind. "Knowledge is NOT culture. The domain of culture begins when one HAS 'forgotten-what-book' " (*GK* 134). So does the domain of reading.

Reading *from* the Pisan cantos

Let us destroy a characteristic passage of the Pisan cantos by supplying backgrounds and connections, by turning it into narrative, by grounding it in realistic psychological discourse. Nothing starts or ends in these cantos, everything flows and is interwoven, but we will arbitrarily begin in the middle of 79/488 ("How is it far if you think of it?") and continue through two-thirds of page 489 ("Kyrie eleison").

In the cantos before the Pisan sequence there are occasional glimpses of an "I" we may call Pound himself: sitting on the Dogana's steps in Venice in 1908, at the opening of Canto 3; visiting a scholar, old Lévy, to discuss a fine point of Provençal philology in Canto 20. Yet these are glimpses in a poem largely impersonal, the poet working through masks or texts, its autobiography – its "growth of a poet's mind" – submerged. In the sequence written during six months in a United States Army prison camp near Pisa in 1945, the reader finds Pound himself at the centre of the action, largely an action within the mind, a drama of memory. Following the Allied invasion of Italy, Pound had been placed under arrest, charged with high treason for his wartime broadcasts over Rome Radio. Isolated first in a steel "gorilla cage" open to the elements, later in a small tent, he is surrounded by the sights and sounds of his prison. Here he comes before us as Old Ez, folding his blankets in the dawn, hearing the sick call list recited.

> The moon has a swollen cheek
> and when the morning sun lit up the shelves and battalions
> of the West, cloud over cloud
>   Old Ez folded his blankets
> Neither Eos nor Hesperus has suffered wrong at my hands
>
>   O Lynx, wake Silenus and Casey
>   shake the castagnettes of the bassarids,
> the mountain forest is full of light
>   the tree-comb red-gilded
> Who sleeps in the field of lynxes
>   in the orchard of Maelids?
> (with great blue marble eyes
>   "because he likes to," the cossak)

Salazar, Scott, Dawley on sick call
    Polk, Tyler, half the presidents and Calhoun
"Retaliate on the capitalists" sd/ Calhoun "of the North"

The blankets, the sick call, take place in a "real" time counterpointed with a timeless world of memory, thought and vision. The two worlds cross or form a Joycean parallax, as a visionary lynx belonging to the god Dionysus/Zagreus (it may also be a prison cat) is told to wake, simultaneously, Silenus, a satyr from the world of myth, and someone we recognize from Canto 74 as one of the prison cadre, Corporal Casey. In memory, the prisoner has been reviewing his life to date. Here he recalls a garden party in London some thirty years ago, where he was in the presence of Lidya, the Princess Bariatinsky, and Henry James. He leaves it to the reader to savour the distance between that garden party in London's Temple and his present company and place of residence. The Princess is remembered

                    holding dear H. J.
        (Mr. James, Henry) literally by the button-hole...
    in those so consecrated surroundings
                    (a garden in the Temple, no less)
                    and saying, *for once*, the right thing
    namely: "Cher maître"
    to his checqued waistcoat, the Princess Bariatinsky,
    as the fish-tails said to Odysseus, ἐνὶ Τρoιη.

The twentieth century and the world of myth cross again, with wry humour, as the Princess is figured as a Siren (fish-tail) seducing the Odyssean American novelist. The Greek tag ("in Troy," *eni Troy-AY*) is from the song of the Sirens in the *Odyssey*. It may act as a semi-private overtone, as well, for Pound had used it in his "farewell to London," *Hugh Selwyn Mauberley*, a poem overtly "Jamesian."

Eos and Hesperus are the planet Venus as morning and evening star. As goddess, Venus appears in both Latin and Greek. (The second Greek word below is one of her titles, Kuthera-Cythera. The first Greek word is Iacchos, one of the names of Dionysus.) Maelids are tree-nymphs. Priapus is a divinity of fertility, in some stories the son of Iacchos-

Bacchus-Dionysus and Venus-Cythera. The cry of "Io!" is "Hail!" — these gods with their attendant lynxes and vegetation are about to appear in an extended, rapturous visionary ritual that bursts forth on the next page and continues to the end of the canto.

> and on the hill of the Maelids
> in the close garden of Venus
> asleep among serried lynxes
> set wreathes on Priapus Ἰακχος, Io! Κύθηρα, Io!
> having root in the equities

The phrase about the cossack, "because he likes to," completes a story begun at the start of the passage, a memory of the Princess's from her youth in Imperial Russia. I don't know if the blue marble eyes are Pound's memory of the Princess or hers of the cossack. Her story may have come to mind just now because the poet is, in a sense, in the charge of American cossacks, who execute some of his fellow prisoners. Many prisoners have the same names as American Presidents; one shares the name of the pre-Civil War Southern politician, John C. Calhoun, a Vice-President. That allows a touch of economic history, even as the ecstatic Dionysian vision — out of history — is gathering energy: we are reminded of the evils of capitalism, and that the Civil War had usurious banking as one of its causes. The phrase about "root in the equities" derives from yet another world, another time, that of Confucius. ("Equities" — fairness, natural justice — is quoted from Pound's own translation of Confucius.) In Pound's universe, the ecstatic sexual experience suggested by Priapus-Iacchos-Cythera has much to do with the roots of justice, whereas, by countermovement, the "religion" of the American missionaries in China (note the sudden flatness of language) is rooted in falsification and greed, *not* in the Confucian equities.

> and you can make 5000 dollars a year
> all you have to do is make one trip up country
> then come back to Shanghai
> and send in an annual report
> as to the number of converts

> Sweetland on sick call
> ἐλέησον   Kyrie eleison

Kyrie eleison, "Lord have mercy." Mercy on Sweetland, who is sick; on the poet, in this prison camp, charged with a capital crime; on us all, who suffer the purgatory of history.

Now the fragments are connected, the names explicated, the Greek translated, the white spaces all filled in. And of course the extraordinary concentration of the verse is lost, as is the fused experience, as close to simultaneity as we can come with words occupying time-space on a page. We may draw generalizations, and they sound boring before we complete the utterance. The pleasure and emotion of the passage comes with its surprises: we have no way of guessing where it will move next, through its remarkable range of subjects, tones and languages. The precision of "The moon — " (if we expect an *O altitudo*, we don't get one) — "The moon has a swollen cheek" is followed by the expansive *un*folding of cadence, image and sky in the following two enjambed lines. That expansion is then suspended, with perhaps an effect of syncopation, as the verse contracts, comes down to earth with Old Ez folding his blankets. How can we describe, *need* we describe — the daring, affectionate confidence with which the language brings together two times, two worlds, two states of mind in "wake Silenus and Casey"? Henry James, a Russian princess, Homer, a cossack, a group of American prisoner-soldiers and John C. Calhoun stand nearby. The best we can hope from the discourse of explication is that some of it may be transmuted as a "forméd trace" in the mind (36/178)

> nothing matters but the quality
> of the affection —
> in the end — that has carved the trace in the mind
> (76/456)

Because the Pisan cantos are for many readers the finest and most moving section of the poem, we should pause to read closely one more brief passage. Observe how times and the languages of times co-exist and play against each other in the following lines from 80/512–13:

with a mind like that he is one of us
       Favonus, vento benigno
       Je suis au bout de mes forces/
That from the gates of death,
    that from the gates of death: Whitman or Lovelace
       found on the jo-house seat at that
in a cheap edition! [and thanks to Professor Speare]
hast'ou swum in a sea of air-strip
    through an aeon of nothingness
when the raft broke and the waters went over me

Here Pound merges, as he does so often, with Odysseus. The first line conjoins the personal and the classical, past and present. Within its simplicity it combines traces of Homer's Greek; the direct language Pound had won through to for translation and poetry between 1912 and 1915; and common speech. Odysseus was *polumetis*, quick-witted, "never at a loss," and the poet at Pisa can only survive by using his god-like Odyssean wits. He is remembering here his own lively translation from the *Odyssey* in *Guide to Kulchur* (146):

And as Zeus said [of Odysseus]: "A chap with a mind like THAT! the fellow is one of us. One of US."

In the Latin "Favonus," the west wind is personified and classicized. It is a "kindly breeze" (vento benigno), a real breeze blowing across the fields of the DTC.

   The next line is a marvelous co-existence of the tragic and comic. Pound is recalling his early years in London, where the eccentric Mme Strindberg, the playwright's widow and proprietress of a "Vorticist" café, was famous for exclaiming (regularly), "Je suis au bout de mes forces" (I am at the end of my powers). The ironic overtone within the memory nicely takes the edge off the genuine despair, for Pound is close to the end of *his* powers − in fact "at the gates of death." He is about to drown like the hero in *Odyssey* V − we will find him drowning again at the end of Canto 95 − his raft broken and the waters coming over him. But this Odysseus is drowning in the nothingness of a career in ruins, his sea made of "air-strip," the metal mesh of a prison cage. Odysseus was saved by the goddess, Leucothea, and her bikini (95/645).

Some unknown soldier-Leucothea saves Pound by leaving behind him in the latrine Speare's *Pocket Book of Verse*. Something to read! And something to make cantos from! Speare's collection of old favorites contributes many echoes and quotations to the Pisan cantos (for example, the ironic "at my grates no Althea" (81/519), echoing another prison-poem, Lovelace's "To Althea"). Speare's immediate contribution, however, is the "hast 'ou" just following his name. It comes from a song by Ben Jonson (in Speare), and appears again as "Hast'ou seen the rose in the steel dust" (74/449).

Jo-house and Lovelace, air-strip and Homer, a cheap edition and an aeon of nothingness, all exist on the same plane within the mind. The *Pisan Cantos*, so firmly anchored to time by their title, are about a poet drowning but *polumetis*, transcending time. "How is it far, if you think of it?" (77/465).

Questions of form

"The perception," M. L. Rosenthal recalls of his first encounters with Pound's verse, "had to come through the poems, not as an abstraction but as sensed magnetic process one was invited to enter" (*Pai* 15.2–3.111). Rosenthal's metaphor adapts Pound's "rose in the steel dust" (74/449 and *GK* 152), fragments of language and experience drawn together by the mind's dynamic magnetisms. Seeing that rose is by no means "natural" or wholly intuitive: one must learn to read the poem. Yet even as it places difficulties in the way, the *Cantos* goes to great lengths to instruct us how and how not to read it, pausing often to point to its own codes. For example, it tells us not to look for a schema (74/444), and that the poet himself has probably erred in thinking that beauty could be "dragged into paradise by the hair" (74/431). The Dantesque scheme of hell-purgatory-paradise, as has been noted, must be seen only as analogy, not as structure, not even as a broken structure: the reader will waste a great deal of energy, as I can testify, trying to decide whether each bit of the poem is "infernal," "purgatorial," or "paradisal."

Critics have argued about whether or not the poem has "major form." All sorts of schemes, charts, patterns and balances have been offered, with the effect of making the *Cantos* seem more orderly than it is. Pound was aware that "major form" was not his strong point. He had not yet produced any work containing a "shining example of Form of the whole," he admitted to Ford Madox Ford in 1932. *Mauberley*, he thought, "has got some structure . . . but I ain't ready to theorize about major form YET" (*PF* 111). In *Guide to Kulchur*, that prose doppelgänger of the *Cantos*, he makes an astonishing, witty and revealing turn on the classical or neo-classical standard of the unities, with their attendant "rules":

Again I reiterate that if my respected pubrs. expect of me, in accord with contract, a chronological exposition, they will have to wait for tables and an appendix. I have no intention of writing one HERE. [The tables or appendix, of course, never appeared.] . . .
   I see no reason why the unities shd. be restricted to greek stage plays and never brought into criticism.   (129–30)

He means that the "unity" of time, place and action occurs within his mind, fashioning disparate knowledge into new "ideogrammic" forms, not through syllogism or chronological sequence, which, for Pound, are distortions of the way we know things.

He never got around to theorizing about major form, nor did he impose one on the *Cantos*. As he added to the poem or came across new materials that interested him, he allowed them to find a place in the expanding code, trusting principally that a dynamic magnetism would hold everything together by the quality of the poet's affection. "The production IS the beloved" (104/742), he wrote in the mid-1950s, and in the final fragments the poem itself is addressed as "M'amour, m'amour" (my love). The best analogy, he thought, always insisting upon it as a loose analogy not to be literalized, was music. "It's music," he told an interviewer in 1968, "Musical themes that meet each other." Themes and counter-themes appear, are repeated, varied, metamorphosed, analyzed into motifs to be developed in new combinations, work by fugue, quotation, contrast, inversion, episode and so forth, without adhering to any pre-existent form or rules of composition. As music, the *Cantos* might be thought closer to a piece like the great *Concord* sonata of Pound's slightly older contemporary, the American composer Charles Ives, than, say, to a piece by Haydn. Pound once made a comparison to Béla Bartók's Fifth Quartet and "as much of Beethoven's music as I can remember," both of which shared as a "record of struggle," the "defects or disadvantages of my Cantos" (*GK* 135).

Codes and conflicts

At innumerable points the *Cantos* offers metaphors for itself, and discusses and questions its own procedures. The poem is many things at once and its multiplicity is its saving grace. Even the title presents a problem of one-and-many, and Pound referred to his text both as single and plural. My sense of it/them as more unified than not, produces a jarring "the *Cantos* is." The poem is an Odyssean voyage, a sailing after knowledge, although it asks "Shall two know the same in their knowing?" (93/631) and is aware of knowledge as "the shade of a shade" (47/236), achieved by indirection: "Our science is from the watching of shadows" (85/543). The voyage proceeds by what Pound calls at several points *periplum* (74/447; 77/466), by which he means taking one's bearings not with a map or chart but improvising from point to point along a coastline. There are shipwrecks (as at the end of Canto 95), miraculous rescues (beginning of Canto 96), and warnings to the reader of dangers ahead (at the end of Canto 109). Sometimes the journey is by land, and the poet can stumble (92/620). The poem is fragmentary (8/28), yet fragments can form a mosaic. It is a labyrinth, a weaving, a spider web, also a pneumatic hammer (Cantos 85–95 are a "Rock-Drill"). On other pages, readers are cast as a jury in a criminal case, addressed by a poet-prosecutor who has been assembling evidence over many years: "Look at the Manchester slums," he sums up, supplying statistics for youth unemployment, adult illiteracy, and a society ridden with violent crime (46/234–35). Yet he moves as well in realms of knowledge where "I have no will to try proof-bringing" (36/177). The text admits to confusion, yet confusion is a necessary "source of renewal" (21/100). Weaving an endless sentence (7/24), the poem neither begins (its first word is "And") nor ends (its final pages are "Drafts and Fragments"). Thundering at us at times with what sounds like dogma, it turns to inveigh against the conformity of dogmatism, which can only be maintained by lies (97/679), urges us to read it as "optative, not dogmatic" (97/668), and considers it a mark of respect if we should find it worth contradicting (114/791). It questions the power in which it placed its hopes – "Litterae nihil sanantes" – writings that cure nothing (106/795). In its final pages it is a set of notes, a tangle, a very small light surrounded by great darkness, and a palimpsest, a text written over other texts, one expecting, asking to be in turn written over (116/795–797).

One might draw up a list of oppositions which, with proper cautions, could be used for decoding much of the *Cantos*. Though helpful, such a list will perforce make the poem sound simplistic or reductive, in part because it points to Pound's Confucian–American moral idealism, which can be seen itself as simplistic. It indicates, too, the rational-didactic impulse in the poet, which allows him to include within a sophisticated and contradictory "open" text statements such as "and with one day's reading a man may have the key in his hands" (74/427). This is Pound as the "village explainer," as Gertrude Stein called him. Burton Hatlen, in an essay on Pound's politics, has discussed the problem of apparently simple ideas within a complex poetics:

Pound thought he had found a new way of bringing these two dimensions of our world together: in the ideogram, concrete particulars could come together to "configure" an idea. In effect, the ideogrammic method rules out any possibility that "meaning" or "truth" might exist *beyond* the particulars, in a Platonic realm of "ideas". . .
Pound himself, I think, was only sporadically aware of the full consequences of his poetic method, for his own comments generally suggest that he saw the ideogram as nothing more than a new way

to communicate ideas . . . The poem "succeeds," I would propose,
precisely because the gap between Pound's particulars and the
general ideas that he intends to communicate to us will *not* close
. . . [T]he particulars refuse to do what he wants them to do; and
the miracle of the poem is that Pound's *method* allows each of these
particulars to retain its own "luminous" life, even as his *will* is trying to force them into a (specious) pattern.   (159–60).

Here, however, if the reader will bear the above in mind as
caveat, are some of the of principal oppositions that form the
poem's code: where we find people making war, manufactur-
ing or selling munitions, we have evil; making or keeping
peace is good. Signs of monopolistic practices and of high
taxes or high interest rates, are opposed to signs of distribution, feeding the people, relief from taxation, low interest, if
any, on loans. Communication, especially across cultural or
linguistic barriers is desirable; whatever impedes communication or obscures texts is not. Awareness, curiosity, are set
against ignorance, cliché, the drag of habit. The poet blesses
those who clarify or codify laws, blasts those who impede the
artist from working freely. Light, clarity, speed, precious
gems, crystal, especially in combination, are signs of the
"paradisal." Gods, who are ambiguous and often hard to
codify, are signs of a "vital universe" with which we should
be in harmony, their presence indicating "magic moments,"
a "bust through the quotidian."

Pound's universe, in spite of his dogmatic outbursts, is
open to experience, qualification and contradiction. The
finer, more delicate side of his mind usually comes along to
keep his loitering or coarser certainties on the move. Thus
myth, as a way of knowing, derives inestimable virtues from
its limitations, for it "knows where to stop, in the sense that
the maker of myth don't try to cut corners, he don't try to
level out all differences" (*GK* 128). The narratives of myth,
that is, refuse to be encapsulated within generalizations or
moral schemes. A code may be useful as long as it remains
"an approximate expression of principles," but when we
forget it is approximation only, and "attempt to square
nature with the code," we find ourselves with perversion of

thought (*GK* 164). Michael André Bernstein argues at length the incompatibility of major axes of the *Cantos* — the diachronic and synchronic, time and the timeless, history and myth — then decides, eloquently, that

Pound's sense of responsibility to each aspect of a contradictory vision, his reluctance to acquiesce in the abolition of either history or myth . . . resulted in some of the finest writing in the *Cantos*, and endowed the poem with an authenticity any arbitrary unity would only have compromised. (107)

Throughout his criticism Pound distinguishes between the constructive and destructive functions of literature, between clearing the ground and new building. We need both acid and building stone, neither of which performs the function of the other (*GK* 88). The *Cantos* takes on both tasks and alternates between them. One of the last things Pound wrote was a memorial for his comrade-in-arms from *Blast* and the Great London Vortex of 1914–15, Wyndham Lewis, whose writings, as with Joyce's *Ulysses*, he always saw as *katharsis*. In Lewis he felt "the intolerable necessity that something come to an end." In contrast, "a decorum has survived, as Vare predicted." "Vare" is the diplomat and popular writer on China, Daniele Varè, whose words, quoted by Pound in a late letter to Lewis, make an appropriate inscription for the *Cantos*: "Empires rise and fall in an epic cycle . . . But ideals do not die" (*PL* 305).

Chapter 2

Instalments

In 1914 Pound abandoned – as too static in its implication – the "image" as a metaphor for poetry, adopting the more dynamic "vortex." Note that the vortex, the poem in motion yet shaped, is primary while "ideas" are secondary: "The image is not an idea. It is a radiant node or cluster; it is what I can, and must perforce, call a VORTEX, from which, and through which, and into which, ideas are constantly rushing" (*GB* 92). Poetry, as Mallarmé said, is not made with ideas, but with words; yet any discussion of the *Cantos* is in danger of allowing the ideas to predominate. The greater my experience with the *Cantos*, the wiser I think Donald Davie's advice that we allow the poem's energies to "interact, climb, spiral, reverse themselves, and disperse," as we listen for "large-scale rhythms" and do not deny ourselves the experience of reading "many at a time, and fast" (*Pound* 84–85). This chapter offers a very swift overview of the poem as it appeared in instalments from 1930 to 1969. Major thematic concerns, and some of the outstanding figures in the poem, are discussed more thoroughly in chapter 3.

A Draft of XXX Cantos (1930)

To what extent did Pound think his poem accessible *as poetry* to readers who would, as it were, enter the vortex? It is difficult not to find unintended irony when in the early 1930s we hear the author of *A Draft of XXX Cantos* lecture a young poet, Louis Zukofsky, on the obscurity of Zukofsky's verse. Poetry demands "concentration / BUT AFTER that you have . . . to go out for the NEXT step / which is clarity /." Zukofsky "cd. have expressed the same subject matter in a more simple and lucid manner without losing one jot of the meaning" (*PZ* 137, 125). The last phrase is curious, for although Pound urges them on Zukofsky, simplicity and lucidity appear as potential threats to meaning. In the *Cantos*, is the meaning to some extent the very difficulty of discovering "meaning"? The confusion of history, our confusion before it, is the matter of the first thirty cantos. These things happened, as people acted, thought and wrote; these are the kinds of things that happen. If we come to discern patterns, fine, but the patterns must not be forced at the expense of contradictions, mysteries, an almost intractable human nature, and a persistent if erratic vision, "flitting / And fading" on "the barb of time" (5/17). We are in a "Wilderness of renewals, confusion / Basis of renewals" (20/92), "Confusion, source of renewals" (21/100).

The poem begins as epics are supposed to, *in medias res*, in the midst of an ongoing story, in the midst of a sentence, "And then . . ." That *And* is the first of well over eight hundred, most of them capitalized, which run down the left-hand margins of these thirty cantos. We need only listen to the cumulative power of those *Ands*, to have much of the meaning. Only a few can be explained as simple conjunctions; only a few are the *ands* of simple temporal sequence. These are the *ands* of a child telling about his or her week at summer camp, all the stories tumbling upon each other without chronology. They form one of the most characteristic sounds of the *Cantos* (observe them in a later canto in the passage from Canto 92 above, p. 18). They are *ands* of metamorphosis, as one thing turns into another. They are *ands* of simultaneity, for all these stories are present in the mind, available to the present at once. These *ands* work in many ways, but taken together they abolish time. How is the mind to make sense of, to deal with, all these things that have formed it, that it is aware of at once?

The first thirty cantos begin with the poet as Odyssean voyager, and with an overlayering of languages – Anglo Saxon, Renaissance Latin, modern American. They take us from Odysseus in the underworld to theophanies of Aphrodite and Dionysus (end of Canto 1 and Canto 2), which would probably have been some "time" before Odysseus; to the twentieth century, as the young Pound sits on the Dogana's steps in Venice; back to a world of gods floating in azure air; briefly to the Cid (eleventh century, the tale taken from a twelfth-century poem); to the murder of Ignez da Castro (fourteenth century); and to Mantegna's fifteenth-century murals in Mantua, seen flaking from a wall in the present. All this, and much more, by the end of the third canto.

As the poem continues we return sporadically to the twentieth century — the poet sitting in meditation, as if watching all these things pass before his eyes in the ruined Roman arena at Verona (4/16; 11/50; 12/53); World War I and the Russian revolution (Canto 16); the young Pound visiting a synagogue in Gibraltar (Canto 22); and many tales, some comic, some not, about the conduct of business, including in Canto 18 the sinister activities of Sir Zenos Metevsky (the thinly disguised munitions magnate and financier, Sir Basil Zaharoff, still active when these cantos were published). We keep leaving the twentieth century, as well — for the China of Confucius (Canto 13); for a Renaissance Venice where art and commercial rapacity thrive, and where the glamour of the Doges' palace hides its stinking dungeons (Cantos 25–26).

The bewildering juxtapositions of "real" pasts and presents can suddenly open onto worlds of myth, visions, states of mind not bound to history, for example in the movement from 1918 at the end of Canto 16 to the metamorphic "magic moment" at the beginning of Canto 17, "So that the vines burst from my fingers"; or the reverse movement from myth — Artemis, Mars and Venus — back into history in the last of the XXX Cantos, with the beautiful lines about King Pedro's love for his murdered queen, and the splendours and squalors of the Borgias. Paradoxes of the Renaissance dominate these cantos, which are a complex image of the human condition in the "Purgatory of error," and which pass beyond our ability to sort things out neatly as good or bad. We are in a poetic universe of changes, transformations, recurrences, where, for example, two beautiful "Helens", Eleanor of Aquitaine and Helen of Troy, merge with each other through puns in Homeric Greek: they are "man-destroying," "city-destroying," the darker side of the powers of Aphrodite (7/24). Note, too, the extraordinary transformations in the marvellous, densely wrought Canto 4, where tales of destructive passion from the lives of troubadours are paired through linguistic magic with tales from Ovid. One theme of the canto is the futilty of attempts to possess the coursing energies of nature, in particular sexuality. The king cannot own the wind; Danaë's father cannot lock her away from Zeus's shower of gold; husbands cannot shut away their wives from troubadour-lovers. An enactment of metamorphosis takes place in this canto through syntax and punctuation: there are almost no "sentences," as everything moves forward on a fluidity of commas and colons, of missing subjects and main verbs. Indeed, the syntax of the *Cantos* as a whole avoids the "properly" punctuated English sentence.

The centrepiece of Renaissance history is formed by the four cantos (8–11) devoted to the life of the *condottiere* and patron of the arts, Sigismundo Malatesta, Lord of Rimini. "No one has claimed that the Malatesta cantos are obscure," Pound wrote. "They are openly volitionist, establishing, I think clearly, the effect of the factive personality, Sigismundo, an entire man" (*GK* 194). After a nasty squabble (8/28) between Truth and the Muse of epic poetry, Calliope, who will never get together except on uneasy terms, we are plunged into a clutter of documents and gossip. Our closest attention will never straighten out this tangle of battles, shifting allegiances, treacheries, assassinations and accusations. Through the documentary fragments we discern the figure of Sigismundo fighting a losing battle to keep his territories and to raise money to pay the artists, scholars and craftsmen he gathered in Rimini. His central effort is towards the building of his Tempio, "a temple so full of pagan works," a monument at once to God, the pagan gods, Renaissance humanism, his beloved mistress and third wife, Isotta, and to his own ego. If Sigismundo was a failure, "he was at all events a failure worth all the successes of his age. He had in Rimini, Pisanello, Pier dell Francesca . . . If the Tempio is a

jumble and a junk shop, it nevertheless registers a concept"
(*GK*, frontispiece). Pound implicitly draws the parallel
between Malatesta and himself, the Tempio and the *Cantos*.
The Tempio was accomplished "outside the then system . . .
against the current of power." A flawed hero, Sigismundo
"registered a state of mind, of sensibility, of all-roundness
and awareness" (*GK* 159).

The section ends on a mysteriously suspended note, as we
hear of the "new birth" of learning in the Renaissance —
represented by the printing and typecutting of Aldous and
Soncinus — and the death, rumoured to be by poisoning, of
a Borgia Pope. At the end of the *XXX Cantos* we may feel
that we can say little beyond the words of Acoetes, "I have
seen what I have seen" (2/9). To which we must add: and
heard what we have heard. For the languages of these cantos,
if we will listen to them, carry the meaning as they alternate
between the archaic and the modern, the documentary and
the lyrical, the sublime and the gutter, all present, brought
together with *Ands*.

Eleven New Cantos (1934)

Themes stated in the first cantos — myth/vision,
history/money, directed will/indifference — find variations
with new subjects and tonalities in Cantos 31–41, which
Pound later titled "Jefferson — Nuevo Mundo." The
predominant flux/metamorphoses of the first thirty cantos
gives way to a greater decidability: we can more easily divide
the figures striving towards light and justice from those who
form or are supporting the forces of darkness. Others are
neither, merely ignorant, misguided or passive within the
purgatory of error. Among the blessed: Thomas Jefferson
and John Adams; three later presidents who fought the
American Bank Wars of the early nineteenth century, John
Quincy Adams, Andrew Jackson and Martin Van Buren;
Marx and Lenin; the poet, Guido Cavalcanti; the
philosopher-theologian, Scotus Erigena; Gandhi; the
economic theorist, C. H. Douglas; and the Italian dictator,

Mussolini. Among the damned: Nicholas Biddle, President of the Second Bank of the United States; American politicians who supported the Bank, Senators John C. Calhoun and the corrupt Daniel Webster; the financiers and/or munitions magnates Metevsky, Mellon, Morgan, Krupp and Schneider; and Churchill (ever a pet dislike of Pound's).

Discussions below of Adams, Cavalcanti and Douglas will examine much of the material in these eleven cantos. On the first page of the section we hear of brave beginnings in a new world, represented by Jefferson; on the final page Jefferson returns to complain that the nation has been "saddled" by banks, and deprived of "Independent use of our money," his words followed by a coda about war and the munitions industry in the twentieth century. This movement is reflected in miniature as we turn from quotations from Marx to suggestions that the Russian revolution, like the American, has not lived up to the Enlightenment intelligence that inspired it (33/162–63). "Out of which things seeking an exit" is twice stated (40/199, 201), as the poem reaches toward the paradisal imagery of high air, the empyrean, the "ineffable crystal" (40/201). Dominated by history, the section is twice interrupted by "Eleusinian" lyrics, Canto 36 (a translation of Cavalcanti) and Canto 39.

In Canto 39 we return to Odysseus, of whom we have heard little since Canto 20: he and his men are in danger of being mired in Circe's "pigsty," from which, of course, the hero's intelligence releases them. Like the poet of whom he is a figure, Odysseus wants to *get* somewhere. The stately vigour of Canto 1, however, is here replaced with much snappier language: "Discuss this in bed said the lady" and Circe's "Been to hell in a boat yet?" The point of Canto 39 is the contrast between the mindless sexuality-sensuality of Circe's island and the ecstatic sexuality of the second half of the canto, accompanied by images of flame and the rebirth of vegetation in a "new spring."

What might have been high historical drama in Canto 37 is rather a disappointment, as the obliquity of Pound's method makes it difficult to understand the details of the

Bank War, to discern who is speaking or the point of the remarks. The canto ends with a tributary epitaph for the "neglected" Martin Van Buren, "Here lies the liberator of the Treasury," but Van Buren remains resistant to heroic treatment. Only after we have prepared ourselves with extensive backgrounds and contexts, can we feel the full weight of the issues. We will return to the Bank War in Cantos 88–89. The "ad interim" with which the section concludes suggests not only that more cantos are to come, but that there remains "in the intellect possible" (36/177) the "way out" the poem is seeking.

The Fifth Decad of Cantos (1937)

In this section the poem achieves a sense of concentration and climax, with three great lyrics, 45, 47 and 49; its celebration of "positive" moments in history in Cantos 41–44; and a certain panache in the impassioned rhetoric of the prosecuting attorney in Canto 46. There are some cryptic historical pages, especially in the Napoleonic material in Canto 50. Of the slack, chatty, anecdotal passages, it might be argued that they offer a lighter "relief" or contrast, as well as reminding us that we live in the twentieth century, surrounded by confusing voices.

One of the pleasures of life is the excitement of productive research, and nowhere else in poetry is that excitement celebrated as in Cantos 42–43. The poet, among ancient books and manuscripts in an Italian archive, finds just what he needs to make his case, the story of the Monte dei Paschi, the Bank of the Pastures (see below, p. 93), a "damn good bank," one founded upon rational principles, but with "soul," as well. There is no single hero behind the long struggle to persuade enlightened monarchs to support the Monte; it is a civic project, one that required persistence and a directed communal will. The otherwise unknown signers of the documents – Pasquini, Gionfiglioli – act in behalf of "the Senate and People of Siena." Based, as it were, upon the guarantee of nature, that is, the productivity of the grazing lands, the Monte addresses problems caused "OB PECUNIAE SCARCITATEM," by the scarcity of money. The bank makes money available to all, taking only the minimal "profit" needed for administration. Yet in the midst of this triumph the poem notes the fragility of individual life and achievement: the wave-like handwriting on one of the documents brings a lyric interruption as the researcher muses, "wave falls and the hand falls / Thou shalt not always walk in the sun" (42/210) — rhythms and tonalities that lead forward to the meditation of Canto 47.

Canto 44 moves rapidly forward in time to another shining moment in Tuscan history, as the Grand Duke Pietro Leopoldo and his son, Ferdinando, bring Enlightenment wisdom to their territories. They abolish imprisonment for debt, the death penalty and torture; support the Monte dei Paschi and distribute grain; accomplish land reform while taxing princes and the church; free printers of censorship and so on. It is at times hard to make out the details without turning to a history of the period, especially when Napoleon — an ambiguous figure in the *Cantos* — enters the picture after his invasion of Italy. Here the emphasis is upon Napoleon as representative of the enlightened aspects of the French Revolution; he pays high tribute to artists, establishes a code of laws, improves farming. Yet Pound cannot forget the destructive side of Napoleon, so "Thank god such men be but few." After a somewhat nervous look at the Napoleonic period in Tuscany, the canto returns to the Leopoldine reforms and the Monte dei Paschi. Canto 44 is filled with the sounds of music and of fireworks going off as the people shout VIVA and EVVIVA in celebration of their enlightened Grand Dukes.

In contrast to the positive achievements celebrated in Cantos 42–44, the famous Canto 45 denounces evil in the figure of Usura (usury), which we will examine in greater detail in the next chapter. The canto's savage chant against Usura is balanced by its desire for the good and the beautiful, for arts, crafts, architecture, wholesome food, love and sex not palsied by greed. The relations among usury, beauty, quality and time are adroitly drawn:

> no picture is made to endure nor to live with
> but is made to sell and sell quickly

In Canto 51 the chant of Canto 45 is repeated in modern English, where it is followed first by a celebration of the union of nature and culture in the craft of tying flies for fishing; then by a brief glimpse into medieval "light philosophy," to the effect that the human mind is godlike and that each of its finer achievements has light "as it were / a form cleaving to it." The canto and the section end with the sudden appearance of Usura's twin, Geryon (Fraud), skilled in disguising his malevolence as virtue.

Canto 47 is a particularly fine mythical-erotic lyric (although from a feminist perspective we must recognize the problems of the strong polarity of male as doer-actor, female as intuitive *genetrix*). Circe sends Odysseus off on the dark voyage with which we began in Canto 1; then the story of Odysseus merges with fertility myths in a lament for Adonis and a modern folk-ritual in which small lights are set out to float at sea. Following a passage on the relative insignificance of the individual life, the canto ends with one of the poem's most profound meditations on mysteries of death, sexuality, cosmic time, re-birth and fertility. Between Cantos 47 and 49 there is the annoying interruption of Canto 48, which seems a miscellany into which the poet has crammed scraps of anecdotes, documents and historical bits — a modern babel among which we can discern familiar themes.

Canto 49 returns to the Confucian serenity of Canto 13 and to a classical anonymity ("by no man these verses"), as if written from the perspective of a recluse's hut set in the midst of a Chinese landscape painting. The peaceful speaker watches the seasons pass, tills his fields, allows himself a moment of anger at state debt, infamy and Geryon, but returns to a serenity in which he asks "Imperial power is? and to us what is it?" The canto concludes in the "dimension of stillness" and shows that for all the differences in tonality it forms a pair with Canto 47, with which it somewhat mysteriously shares its final words, "the power over wild beasts."

Cantos LII–LXXI (1940)

Time and space in the *Cantos* have no fixed principles, expanding, contracting and bending within the text. The Pisan cantos, especially, are a virtuoso exercise in metamorphoses of time. In the twenty Cantos 52–71, time is what the poet makes it: ten cantos on Chinese, ten on John Adams and American history, each set occupying almost exactly the same amount of space. Yet the China cantos embrace some five thousand years; the Adams cantos about thirty. Language and allusion swing us wildly through time and place. Within the China cantos there are traces of Aeschylus and the *Odyssey*, medieval philosophy, Cavalcanti, Valturio (a Renaissance engineer), Jefferson and Adams, Cavour, submarines and Mussolini. Call it collage or overlayering, the juxtaposition China/America modifies each world by the other, and both are shaped at times into a loose allegory in support of the Italian régime, for which Pound had become a fervent supporter and propagandist by the late 1930s, when he wrote these cantos. The rapid survey of Chinese history breaks off as the American Revolution begins.

The structure of the first of the China cantos mirrors in reverse the abrupt movement from the Confucian peace of Canto 13 to the noisy hell of Canto 14. The section beings with a presumably "Dantesque" anger over financiers, "jews" (see chapter 4), neschek (usury), Stalin, international sanctions against Italy after the invasion of Abyssinia, and the Church – fat, groggy and toothless – which accepts the usury it once denounced. Suddenly, "Know then:" takes us into a poetic microclimate derived from the *Li Chi*, an ancient almanac of ceremonies and seasons. Pound deals freely with the *Li Chi*, making of it a world where nature and culture are in harmony, semi-divine emperors and empresses mediate between earth and heaven, and formality of manners accompanies observation of plants, animals and constellations. A pre-scientific observation, of course, for "now sparrows, they say, turn into oysters." The verse moves between the stately and the supple. One line which refers literally to nature

can be taken as a moral reading of the Chinese history to
follow, indeed of all history and of the *Cantos*: "Strife is between light and darkness."

The chronicle begins in pre-history with the mythic first
emperors, Yao, Chun and Yu, who invent the arts of civilization. We hear their names invoked with that of Confucius
some millenia later by the first Manchu emperor, Tai Tsong
(58/320), a 'barbarian'' who adopts the best of Chinese
culture, as does each new dynasty as it arrives to take over
from a decadent one. And each becomes decadent in turn, as
its emperors and bureaucracy (usually "eunuchs") fall into
luxurious self-indulgence or the trivial distractions of a "jazz
age HI-TSONG [high song?] (55/292). They indulge in
nepotism, forget the needs of the people, or turn to "foreign"
cultures, in particular Buddhism and Taoism and their attendant superstitions. Pound cannot abide Buddhism or Taoism
(nor most manifestations of Christianity), philosophies which
he sees as drawing us away from social order. The larger
lesson to be learned from Chinese history is that good
emperors and ministers follow Confucian principles, and bad
ones don't. This is intended as a lesson for us all, but especially for Mussolini and his state. For governments and dynasties
take their "mandate" from the people (58/322), and fall
"from losing the law of Chung Ni / (Confucius)" (56/308).
This is an ominous note, for it is the accusation Pound will
bring against himself and Mussolini − or at least Mussolini's
government − five years later in the *Pisan Cantos*, after the
fall of the Fascist regime. At one point the Duce and/or the
Italian people are addressed directly; "TSONG of TANG put
up granaries / somewhat like those you want to establish"
(55/298). The emperor Yong Tching (61/334–39) is clearly
Mussolini in mandarin costume.

Few readers have found the Chinese or Adams cantos
successful. (I defer a discussion of the Adams cantos to the
section on Adams in chapter 3.) They were written rapidly,
when Pound was most distracted by political propaganda,
interpreting world affairs as an effort by international finance
to crush Mussolini, who, Pound thought, threatened its

hegemony. Over the years I have come to find greater pleasure in these cantos, and that is in direct proportion to my ability to give up hoping I could learn Chinese or American history from them. As usual, the poem includes hints about how to read it, and I take the China/Adams section as "less a work of the mind than of affects" (59/324). Buried within it are many beautiful or witty lines, aphorisms and curious anecdotes, moving along on ever-changing registers of speech. Yet it is difficult to read these cantos slowly, and on fast reading the eye is tempted to skip. The concluding twenty lines of the Chinese cantos, however, are very finely wrought: an emperor ("literary kuss") pays tribute to his mother, a great empress who had entered the palace as "a young lady merely of talents." Consider the placement of "merely" within the passage. The canto ends on a delicately ironic note of suspension, leading us away from the poem: "Perhaps you will look up his verses." Even in a time of trouble, as war approached and Pound was more concerned with propaganda than poetry, he had not entirely lost touch with his craft.

The Pisan Cantos (1948)

Few other than the FBI were listening, certainly not seriously, to Pound's wartime radio speeches. He did not think them treasonable; the government saw the matter differently. As American troops fought their way up the Italian peninsula in 1945, they brought with them his name as that of a wanted person. From late May to early November, imprisoned at the Army's Disciplinary Training Center (DTC) near Pisa, he wrote these eleven cantos. They are about a poet saving his sanity: they are also the instrument by which he saved it. The Pisan sequence transformed a floundering poem, as well, for without it the *Cantos* might well appear today merely a curiosity of literary modernism. Neither imprisonment, nor the collapse of his world, nor overtly autobiographical verse had been part of Pound's plan. As Michael Alexander suggests, it is the very adventitiousness, the way Pound rises to the disastrous occasion, that brings life to the poem: "If the *Cantos* change thus untidily from a work with a plan to a work that once had a plan, the inconvenience to our expectations is compensated for by the moving quality of much of what remains" (194).

As we have seen in passages from Cantos 79 and 80, fragments of life in the DTC run counterpoint to the poet's memories and interior reverie. His fellow prisoners are soldiers charged with felonies such as rape and murder, although one of them protests that he "Ain' commited no federal crime, / jes a slaight misdemeanor" (80/493). Convicted prisoners are executed in the DTC, and Pound fears he may be among them. It is forbidden to speak to the poet-prisoner, and when anyone does, the level of conversation is not high. Two soldiers, one black, one white, find him in the shade behind the latrine. The former

> addresses me: Got it *made*, kid, you got it made.
> White boy says: do you speak Jugoslavian? (80/506)

His only reading matter is a Bible, the armed services edition of *Time* magazine, copies of Confucian texts and a Chinese dictionary he had slipped into his pocket when arrested. He considers himself fortunate to discover Speare's *Pocket Book of Verse* (a collection that forty years later one could still purchase). He immediately finds use for it in the poem he is writing, mixing poems from the English and American tradition with the larger text of his memories.

Although they move swiftly, and often secretly, from one association to another, the Pisan cantos are no more a literal "stream of consciousness" than is the mimesis of thought in *Ulysses*. As the learned, witty Joyce has carefully arranged the minds of Stephen, Bloom, and Molly, so has Pound arranged that of the figure who appears as E.P., Old Ez, and "ego scriptor." There is a logic of association, but no scheme. Like Odysseus adrift on his raft, the mind moves "as the winds veer." " 'Spirit veni' / adveni," he asks, but "not to a schema" (74/443–44). He invokes a "femina" (whom I take to be Venus/beauty) "that wd / not be dragged into paradise by the hair'' (74/41). The Pisan cantos are eventful, and often the events are gathered in extended passages such as the memories associated with Spain at 81/517–19, or the visionary ceremonies of Dionysus, Persephone and Venus at 79/489–92. But there is no clear plan or progression, unless we wish to trace a very large but inconstant movement from the turbulence with which the sequence begins − the death of Mussolini and a dream ending "with a bang, not a whimper" − to the Confucian calm achieved in Canto 83. In Canto 84, the conclusion to the sequence, there is relative peace and balance. The final page is governed by a large *chung*[1] 中 − the Confucian balance or "unwobbling pivot." The section concludes with a formal rhymed couplet which has the effect of ambiguous closure:

> If the hoar frost grip thy tent
> Thou wilt give thanks when night is spent.

It is October, and nights are getting chilly at Pisa. Those nights end, but whether the larger night is "spent" remains in question.

Sights and sounds of the DTC punctuate the reverie of "an old man (or oldish)," a "man on whom the sun has gone down": the Stars and Stripes in the breeze, the arrival of a staff car, music played over loudspeakers, bits of language overheard, a marching cadence, "*Hot   hole   hep   cat.*" Sometimes he receives small kindnesses, gifts from the natural world or from Mr Edwards, a black soldier who comes like Kuanon, Chinese goddess of mercy, breaking regulations to make a table for the aging poet: "doan you tell no one / I made you that table" (74/434). Nature sustains him:

> When the mind swings by a grass-blade
>   an ant's forefoot shall save you
> the clover leaf smells and tastes as its flower (83/533)

He observes clouds over Pisa, stars and planets, a dwarf morning-glory, birds, crickets, ants, a lizard, a spider, a cat. The observation is very close:

> And now the ants seem to stagger
>> as the dawn sun has trapped their shadows
>>> (83/531)

He watches a wasp build her "tiny mud-flask" nest, makes a note of how long it takes her to complete it, commenting "and that day I wrote no further" (83/533). This is a marvellous transformation of romantic love into a love of nature, for the reference is to Dante's story of Paolo and Francesca, whose passion overcame them as they read a book − "And that day we read no further."

Memories and anecdotes crowd upon him: from a boyhood in America, youthful visits to Spain, years in London, Paris, Italy, walking tours in the South of France; friendships with Yeats, Joyce, Eliot and many others; women he has loved − H. D.; his wife, Dorothy; Olga Rudge; his daughter, Mary. He sends one of them his thoughts:

> O white-chested martin, God damn it,
>> as no one else will carry a message,
> Say to La Cara: amo.   (76/459)

Because there is no one to converse with, he talks with spirits. Other remembered companions are Confucius, Dante, Adams, paintings, sculptures, beloved churches, music and poems. Now − with a memory of Cavalcanti's canzone in Canto 36:

>> nothing matters but the quality
> of the affection −
> in the end − that has carved the trace in the mind
> dove sta memoria [*where memory lives*]   (76/457)

An examination of conscience takes place: he has been a "hard man in some ways"; has had compassion for others, but probably not enough "and at moments that suited my own convenience"; has spoken too much and lost the law of Confucius (see below, p. 104). There are hints of preparation for confession and − through the words of François Villon − a cry for absolution. Other ceremonies and rituals are suggested, including John of the Cross's dark night of the soul and a spiritual death and rebirth. These cantos are filled with tears, as well as with high comedy and wit.

There are passages that hover ambiguously between the hallucinatory and the mystical; those that focus on eyes of composite goddesses or spirits form a broken story-line. Spirits, souls, persons, essences – he does not know what to call them – suddenly appear before him at 76/452 and 459. In the second half of Canto 81, one of the most intense passages in the poem, they return as stronger presences, staring at him with "unmasked eyes in half-mask's space." Later, in Canto 83, there is a mysterious moment of *atasal*, a word Pound had defined in the essay on Cavalcanti as "Sufi doctrine of union" (*LE* 186):

> The eyes, this time my world,
>   But pass and look *from* mine
>   between my lids
>   sea, sky, and pool

There are also hallucinatory/mystical appearances of pagan gods and goddesses, notably in the celebration of lynxes and pomegranates in Canto 79. It is not quite the case that "the drama is wholly subjective" (74/430), yet "nothing will happen that will / be visible to the sargeants" (78/483).

The drama is both subjective and objective. If events occur within memory and "the timeless air," they also occur within the "real" time of the DTC and the news – often of the deaths of friends – that comes with *Time* magazine. The many "times" are set in counterpoint:

> some minds take pleasure in counterpoint   (79/485)

Times of history, myth, art, nature and one man's life are set against each other, allowing remarkably quick movements of language and mood. Something that happens in any one of these times may be happening in two or three others. These transformations may be seen in the passages from the *Pisan* sequence discussed above (pp. 23–27). Among fragments and images of things broken, the poet-prisoner dreams of rebuilding the fallen ideal city "now in the mind indestructible" (74/430), "now in the heart indestructible" (77/465).

Rock-Drill (1955) and *Thrones* (1959)

What are known as the "later" cantos (85–109) were written during thirteen years of confinement in a Federal hospital for the insane in Washington, to which the court had remitted the poet when he was found mentally unfit to stand trial. Under the circumstances, which were grim, Pound was treated humanely at St Elizabeths, allowed many visitors, and had access to almost any book he wanted. Unlike the dramatic Pisan sequence, the later cantos rarely acknowledge the material conditions under which they were written, that is, in "this bughouse" (105/747). At one point an inmate called Yo-Yo asks the question more subtly raised by Eliot's "Tradition and the Individual Talent" in 1919, "What part ob yu iz deh poEM??" (104/741). If the prolific writings of Pound's Washington years are more cryptic than ever, they also include some of his finest verse. The reader's first impression is of increased white space on the page and of a greater reliance upon typography for phrasing and speed. In the musical analogy Pound encouraged, we might hear these cantos as a *mélange* of fugue and fantasia, and mark them *con brio*, sometimes *con espressione*.

Subjects pass quickly, often stated by the briefest annotation. Although increasingly challenged, the reader who has come this far will be be familiar if not with the subjects, at least with the methods. The verse snaps among languages – English, Greek, Latin, Chinese, even hieroglyphics – and moves from the exalted – "for the kindness, / infinite, / of her hands (108/764) – to the mundane " 'Which is all nuts' said Apollonius" (94/640). The pleasure of this text is in its unpredictable movements of language and recombinations of fact and vision, objective and subjective, classics and gossip, documentary and lyric, clarity and obscurity. One searches with difficulty for linguistic units or punctuation that allow a traditional English sentence: Fenollosan "continuous light-bands" and Ovidian metamorphosis redefine syntax.

After completing the China/Adams cantos in 1940, Pound thought he was finished with his economic work and that the

poem would now emphasize the "positive," moving toward
"philosophy or my 'paradise'," indicated by the names
Dante, Cavalcanti and Scotus Erigena. (*L* 328, 331, 334). The
later cantos are not a "paradise," but they distinctly look to
the empyrean. The last line of *Thrones* is Dante's warning to
his readers in the second canto of the *Paradiso*: "You in the
dinghy (piccioletta) astern there!" Dangerous waters ahead,
says Dante-Pound, many should consider turning back, only
"you other few" who seek the higher realms of knowledge
should follow.

The warning might well have been placed at the beginning
rather than the end of these late cantos, which contain some
splendid lines and passages and direct us toward many interesting subjects, but which are for the Poundian initiate.
Explication is baffled by proliferation of subject, brevity of
allusion and the obliquity with which, to paraphrase Yeats,
these cantos play upon a ghostly paradigm of texts. Terrell's
Companion offers 250 pages of annotation, and elsewhere
several pages have been devoted to a single ideogram, the
great *ling*^{2} that stands at the entrance to *Rock-Drill* (Kearns
196–99). We can do little more than mention the predominant
subjects as they appear.

Cantos 85–86 return to the legendary history of the earlier
China cantos. Drawn from the Confucian "History Classic,"
the *Chou King*, they concentrate on the Chou dynasty, which
Confucius held as exemplary. The *Chou*, like all Confucian
history, is less a record of events than a search for wisdom.
By the 1950s – with the help of translations and Mathews'
great dictionary – Pound had improved his ability to look at
the ideograms, and he hopes to interest the reader in them. In
a note at the end of Canto 85 he claims that the meaning is
"usually" given in the English text. Perhaps it is, but it is
hard to know which English words are connected with which
ideograms. Within this text that moves toward graphic art,
there are some sharply phrased anecdotes and aphorisms,
such as Brancusi's remark on the use-value of time, and
"Awareness restful & fake is fatiguing" (85/558–59).

The pattern of Cantos 52–71, China/America, is "rhymed"

in *Rock-Drill*, for as Pound returns to ancient China in 85–86, so he returns to American history in 88–89. A fresh point of view and new tonalities are provided by the principal source, Senator Thomas Hart Benton's *Thirty Years' View*, an extensive memoir of his public career from 1820 to 1850. Benton was Andrew Jackson's chief ally in the struggle to gain control of the nation's money, which came to a crisis when the charter of the Second Bank of the United States came up for renewal. There is high drama in the story − corruption, machinations, heroism and cowardice − yet we only discover that drama when we read about this chapter of American history elsewhere.

The other *Rock-Drill* cantos are often lyrical, with suggestions of the poet's anguish and exultation, the rapid alternation of emotions captured in the opening of Canto 95, "LOVE, gone as lightning, / enduring 5000 years." Consider the passage at 93/628, beginning "The autumn leaves blow from my hand," continuing with prayers for compassion, then arriving at anguished confession (in French): "I have had compassion for others. Not enough! Not enough!" The verse moves swiftly towards a Confucian meditation, where light is "almost solid." The increasing imagery of light, crystal and velocity in these pages is unmistakable. The precarious position of poet and poem are dramatised on the final page of *Rock-Drill*, in the shipwreck of Pound-Odysseus. Poem and poet do not drown, however, for the sea-goddess Leucothea comes to the rescue. In Homer she throws him her *kredemnon*, her veil, but in Pound she says, "My bikini is worth yr / raft" (95/645). Lines such as that prevent irritation from entirely getting the better of us.

"Yes, my Ondine," Pound remarks at 93/623, "it is so god-damned dry on these rocks." *Thrones* presents an even stonier path than *Rock-Drill*. Canto 96 begins with material from an eighth-century *History of the Langobards* by Paul the Deacon. Once again we are in confusing purgatorial history. The latter half of the canto derives from an obscure *Eparch's Book*, a legal document in Byzantine Greek, promulgated by Leo the Wise (866–912). With minute attention to detail, it demonstrates how a wise government can regulate the affairs of the marketplace to prevent merchants and moneychangers from falsifying standards, and so on. A nineteenth-century *History of Monetary Systems* by Alexander del Mar, for whose works Pound's enthusiasm was great, provides the technical, incomprehensible notes on coinage and gold-silver ratios in Canto 97. The next two cantos are from a Chinese *Sacred Edict*, a set of maxims by a seventeenth-century Manchu emperor, rewritten in "colloquial language" by a salt-commissioner, and ultimately turned into a textbook designed to teach Chinese to Protestant missionaries. The distance between the *Sacred Edict* and the Confucian classics is manifest. Worthy platitudes — "Feed the people"; "don't pester scholars"; the human race is a tribe and should behave as brothers — are only occasionally spiced with wit or interesting phrasings.

A list of new figures and texts appearing in *Thrones* would be long. They include the *Enneads* of Plotinus; the poetic theology of St Anselm; and the life of Apollonius of Tyana, a first-century wandering guru, as recorded or invented by Philostratus at the request of a Byzantine empress. Some attractive passages, to be continued in *Drafts and Fragments*, are inspired by the writings of Joseph Rock, a botantist who lived for years in southwest China, observing the vegetation and landscape, and recording the myths and ways of life of the Na Khi people. A major subject in Cantos 108–109 is Sir Edward Coke (1552–1634), Queen Elizabeth's attorney general, later a leader of the parliamentary revolt against the Crown. Coke's *Institutes* of the Common Law had been cited by John Adams, entering the ideology of the American Revolution.

Pound stated clearly the intention, the central magnetism, of the later cantos:

I have made the division between people dominated by emotion, people struggling upwards, and those who have some part in the divine vision . . . The thrones in the *Cantos* are an attempt to move out from egotism and to establish some definition of an order possible or at any rate conceivable on earth . . . *Thrones* concerns the states of mind of people responsible for something more than their personal conduct.

This is a mature statement of the nobility of purpose and epic aspiration with which he had begun the poem four decades earlier. The method of *Thrones* does not achieve the purpose, although there is what Michael Alexander calls a "splintered beauty" in passages presenting the poet's state of mind, his exultation set against impending darkness, and his intuition of a universe in which there is, as Santayana is quoted as saying at 95/646, "Something *there*." Too often Pound has not lived long enough with his new sources to make them his own. He developed enthusiasm for books, took notes as he read, then made cantos from the notes. In his final period of discouragement, he came to accept the criticism of his friend, Basil Bunting, that too often the *Cantos* do not present, they refer. What is surprising is how many lines and passages, in spite of the failure of the later cantos, catch one's interest or come to take their place in memory.

Drafts and Fragments of Cantos (1969)

At the lowest ebb of his fortunes Pound had saved his poem with the cantos written at Pisa. So, two decades later, another personal crisis produced the *Drafts and Fragments* that arrive to rescue the poem which comes close to drowning in *Rock-Drill* and *Thrones*. Not long after returning to Italy in 1958 old age overtook him; he found he was unable to concentrate for long. It was clear that whatever conclusion he planned for the *Cantos* would not be written. He fell increasingly into long silences, and when he spoke it was often to criticize his poem as harshly as any critic has done. It was a "botch," he said. "I picked out this and that thing that interested me, and then jumbled them together into a bag. But that's not the way to make − a *work of art*." The best the poet could do to conclude the poem was to incorporate within it a recognition of his failures. In the late 1960s some final *Drafts and Fragments* were assembled, perhaps less by Pound than by his publisher, and with the help of friends. The section contains four cantos presented as complete − 110, 113, 114, and 116 − and others marked "from" or "notes for." The final pages, in the original volume, consisted of three short fragments headed "Notes for CXVII et. seq." − an *et sequitur* reaching beyond the boundaries of the text.

The confession of failure is, paradoxically, a bravura gesture of technique and spirit. Some critical discussions of Pound quote phrases on the failure of the poem without listening to the delicate balances, the muted celebrations that accompany them. Readers who know little of Pound or the *Cantos* are likely to have heard, through reviews of biographies, "My errors and wrecks lie about me," "I cannot make it cohere," and "the dreams clash / and are shattered." Yet these phrases exist within a complex image of a mind seeking serenity, guardedly proud of its achievements, sending a life work off to its dubious future, and preparing even wittily for death:

> . . . some climbing
>   before the take-off   (116/796)

There is a subtle drama in the final cantos and fragments, an emotional dialectic that will not be accommodated by the phrase "confession of failure." There is at last a limpidity in these pages; even where we find references we cannot identify and suspect hidden resonances, we are guided adequately by the verse.

Canto 110 begins in a "quiet house." It is in Venice, and water is striking the sea-wall with "paw-flap, wave-tap." Landscapes that seem both real and magical, of this earth and infused with myth, are drawn from observation and transmuted from Rock's Na Khi "world that he saved us for memory" (113/786). There are fragments of Na Khi language, an impenetrable otherness. (The fragment "from 112" is almost entirely Na Khi material.) Goddesses are present: Artemis (Greek), Kuanon (Chinese), Awoi (Japanese), and the Virgin (in mosaic in her "quiet house," a Byzantine church on the island of Torcello, near Venice). "Quos ego Persephonae" (780) is an echo of the Latin poet Propertius:

"There will be three books at my funeral, which I will bring to Persephone, not a trifling gift." "Stop!" says a Chinese ideogram, to which the poet adds "not with jet planes."

Images of serenity, kindness, mercy and nature predominate in Canto 113 and "from 115," an epitaph for Wyndham Lewis. Yet serenity still contends with the old "grumpiness," and is interrupted by memories from purgatorial history and irrepressible impulses to lecture on interest rates. The drama is in allowing serenity to get the upper hand. Moods alternate swiftly (see the passage from Canto 113 on page 4). The poet sees himself as a 'blown husk that is finished," and immediately adds, "but the light sings eternal." The serenity is fragile, a flickering candle "versus this tempest," the light shadowed by memories of troubled personal relationships, and the mind "as Ixion, unstill, ever turning."

In Canto 116 meditations on error and failure to "make it cohere" are set against assertions of achievement and intention. We are reminded of the "turn" in Canto 81, following the passage on vanity: "But to have done instead of not doing / this is not vanity." The poet has brought "a little light" into encircling darkness, affirmed the "gold thread in the pattern"; it is possible to separate the beauty from the madness, to "confess wrong with losing rightness." Beyond the subjective mind, there is a universe that coheres, "even if my notes do not cohere," a splendour to which Pound-Dante's small "rushlight" may "lead back." The alternation continues into the final fragment, which begins with a failure ("faillite"), moves to a memory of larks flying upward from a field, then to a bird falling ("es laissa cader") – but "de joi sas alas" [with joy, his wings]. Canto 116 ends with resonances from two great companions, Dante and Confucius (see the discussion of "flow thru" on p. 62). No long poem has ended on a line more central to its ethos and intention – "To be men not destroyers," an infinitive phrase left for the reader to complete.

Chapter 3

Representative figures

The only American literary ancestor Pound recognizes is Whitman. He ignores Emerson, consciously at least, who for him and his fellow cosmopolitan exile, Eliot, represented vagueness, gentility and other aspects of American culture from which they wished to distance themselves. Yet Emerson's subtle prefatory chapter in *Representative Men* reflects much of the spirit behind Pound's selection of exemplary figures for the *Cantos*: "Other men are lenses through which we read our own minds. Each man seeks those of different quality from his own . . . seeks other men, and the *otherest*." The varied heroes and heroines in the *Cantos* are an assembly of men and women (the latter much less prominent, but many), each irreducibly of his or her time, yet each a conduit for energies of intelligence and affection with which the "vital universe" is charged. I have taken eight names as crossings through which major themes may be examined: the Chinese sage, Confucius; an American orientalist, Ernest Fenollosa; the Latin poet, Ovid; a medieval philosopher, Scotus Erigena; the late medieval poet, Cavalcanti; an amateur British moral economist, C. H. Douglas; the second American president, John Adams; and the Italian dictator, Mussolini. They are lenses through which the poet reads his own mind, yet they provide the necessary difference and otherness. An odd assembly, perhaps, they represent the positive values within the *Cantos*.

Confucius: ethics and moral history

The matter of China enters the poem early, in Canto 4, as a flattering poet, Sō-Gyoku (fourth century BC), maintains that the wind in the palace curtains is not one the king shares with the people; but King Hsiang rejects the proposition that he can own the wind. The anecdote invites allegory: forces of nature should not become sources of individual profit, although the sharp move of the usurer is to convince us that something belonging to all belongs to *him*. Twelve lines later, Père Henri Jacques, a French Jesuit, longs to speak with Chinese spirits of the air on a sacred mountain, Rokku. Eighty-four cantos later, we know he has achieved his desire, for he "still / speaks with the sennin on Rokku" (82/582). Père Henri is clearly free from the exclusivity and fanaticism Pound hated in institutionalized religion.

In Canto 13 Kung (Confucius) walks peacefully into the poem, with his disciples, the sound of the verse itself a reproach to the noisy Western circles of greed, sharp practice and disorder that surround this canto:

> And Kung said, "Without character you will
> be unable to play on that instrument
> Or to execute the music fit for the Odes.
> The blossoms of the apricot
> blow from the east to the west,
> And I have tried to keep them from falling."

Pound's adaptations from the Confucian scriptures in Canto 13 combine a decorous formality with directness and simplicity and we hardly notice the presence of colloquial American speech, "the old swimming hole." Tenets of Confucian ethics are suggested: modesty, wisdom rooted in knowledge of human nature, an order that begins within the individual and moves in ever-widening circles outward into society and the state. Kung's rejection of useless metaphysical-theological speculation is indicated by "And said nothing of the 'life after death'." For Pound, the Christian

concentration or emphasis on eternity is not social. The sense of responsibility, the need for coordination of individuals expressed in Kung's teaching differs radically from early Christian absolutism and from the maritime adventure morals of Odysseus or the loose talk of argumentative greeks.   (*GK* 38)

What paradise we can know occurs on earth, if sporadically,

and (echoing Whitman) "will never be more now than at present" (74/435). The human obligation is not to sit like Yuan
Jang passively receiving wisdom, but to "Get up and do
something useful." Confucius's central teaching, written on
the legendary bo leaves, about the need for inner order and
balance as a prerequisite to useful achievement is presented:

> And Kung said, and wrote on the bo leaves:
>   If a man have not order within him
> He can not spread order about him
>
> . . .
>
>   And if the prince have not order within him
> He can not put order in his dominions.   (13/59)

This is the root from which all Confucian teaching grows; it
forms the first chapter, which "you may treat as a *man-
tram*," of the classic Pound called the *Ta Hio* or *Great
Digest*. When Eliot, in grand Anglican mode, scouting out
heretics and protestants, wanted to know in the early 1930s
what Mr Pound believed, the answer was, "I believe the *Ta
Hio*." Confuian ethics are everywhere in the *Cantos*.

Canto 34 marks the first tentative appearance of the
Chinese ideogram. The lyrical Canto 49 is more Taoist than
Confucian, although Pound was probably unaware of the
nature of the poems and paintings he was working from:
Taoism and Buddhism, neither of which he bothered to look
into very deeply, are always negative signs in the *Cantos*.
Canto 49 is one of those moments at which Pound, busy digg-
ing around in history, cutting and pasting from documents,
almost seems to be pausing for a demonstration that he can
still produce the "effortlessly" beautiful if he wishes:

> Autumn moon; hills rise about lakes
> against sunset
> Evening is like a curtain of cloud,
> a blurr above ripples; and through it
> sharp long spikes of the cinnamon,
> a cold tune amid reeds.
> Behind hill the monk's bell
> borne on the wind.

A large, particularly handsome ideogram introducing Cantos 52–71 announces a major return to Confucian themes. Pages from the *Li Chi*, a magical almanac of rites and seasons, receive a beautiful treatment in Canto 52, as lyric introduction to the nine cantos on Chinese history.

The chronicle of these cantos — seemingly endless, yet swift for the forty-six centuries it covers — observes the presence or absence of Confucian sensibility as dynasties rise and fall, good and bad emperors and ministers succeed each other, order and disorder contend across vast spaces of time. China, like the west, exists within the purgatory of history. When the spirit of Confucian ethics is ignored, the results are manifest:

> . . . the emperor amused himself in his park
>   had a light car made, harnessed to sheep
> The sheep chose which picnic he went to,
> ended his days as a gourmet. Said Tchang, tartar:
>   Are not all of his protégés flatterers?
>   How can his country keep peace?
> And the prince Imperial went into the cabaret business
>   and read Lao Tse.
> HOAI TI was deposed, MIN TI taken by tartars   (54/282)

That the prince reads Lao Tse, the founder of Taoism, and not Confucius, is a bad sign. Yet Confucian harmony, generosity and order periodically rise again, and we hear of emperors who live and speak with simplicity, write poetry, distribute grain to the people, keep down taxes and the price of food, and dying tell their heirs to "Keep the peace, care for the people." "Kung is to China as is water to fishes" (54/285).

In 1927 Pound published his first translation of the *Ta Hio*, but translating at that time meant working from a nineteenth-century French version. In the following decade, however, he began to study Chinese, for the "Immediate Need of Confucius" became more pressing (*SP* 75–80:*89–94*). Working with bilingual texts, glossaries and the authoritative Mathews dictionary, which he suspected he was the only person after its proofreader to have read from cover to cover, he became increasingly able to scrutinize Chinese characters. Being

Pound, ever making it new and reading with *chien*[4], the "luminous eye" (93/629), he thought he saw within the texts patterns and actions scholars had missed. During the Second World War, he published versions in Italian, posted Confucian mottos on the walls of Rapallo, and in late 1945 at Pisa, made fresh English translations. A finer and more vital Confucian English informs the Pisan cantos. The study continued and deepened in Washington, culminating in translations of the 305 Confucian *Odes* and in new ways of reading and writing Chinese for the later cantos.

Rock-Drill begins emblematically with the large, complex *ling*[2], announcing the aspiration of the later cantos as they attempt an ascent towards paradise. Yet the meaning of the ideogram pales in dictionary definitions and abstract English equivalents ("sensibility," "benevolence"). By this time Pound is deeply immersed in Chinese textuality, and he expects the reader, too, to define *ling*[2] as Chinese chracters are in fact defined within the classic texts, by allowing it to accrue meaning through the totality of interactions with its contexts (it appears eight times). One can read the later cantos as a sorting out of those representative figures who display at least some portion of *ling*[2], and those who don't.

Pound's confidence in working directly with Chinese characters is evident in Cantos 85–86, in the freedom with which he dashes through the *Shu*, the *History Classic*, ancient documents traditionally said to have been preserved by Confucius himself. On at least one page, Chinese ideograms and their transliterations far outnumber English words. At times Pound dares to write *in* Chinese, reassembling ideograms in ways that do not appear in the classic texts. The theme of "preservation of documents" is prominent, not motivated by antiquarianism, but as materials for a moral history. Pound-Kung believes that "the basic principles of government are found in the Shu," as in other records of law and government. Confucianism in the later cantos is timeless: bits from the *Shu* occupy the same plane as references to medieval philosophers, Homer, Brancusi, and figures from mid twentieth-century politics. At one point of extremely confident writing, China *c.*1000 BC and the United States 1955 are one, as within the same linguistic space the Emperor Mou Wang, instructing a new minister, and the prophet Ezra, addressing his fellow citizens, each concerned with lineage and law, simultaneously say, "Live up to your line / and the constitution" (86/562). This is less forced than one might think, for the authority of Mathews' dictionary supports the translation of the ideogram, *hsien*, as "constitution." Truths appear timeless, as do the other "Confucian" virtues and moral tags discerned in what English we can read among these pages that look like wall posters: cultivate charity, solicitude, awareness; laws should not be oppressive; "Get the mot juste before action"; beware a loveless heart . . .

From Canto 85 to the end of the poem, Confucian tonalities permeate the text. The final concentration of Chinese materials is in Cantos 98–99, which are saturated with ethical instruction about simplicity of manners, the responsibility of rulers and people, harmony with nature, and the "filial" respect that should inform society. In his later years Pound had become so thoroughly immersed in Confucian thought that it informs the poetry even at points where the reader hardly suspects its presence. At the end of the last complete canto, 116:

> Charity I have had sometimes,
> > I cannot make it flow thru.

"Flow thru" takes a resonance from *Analects* 15.2.2., where Kung talks of his unified awareness of the "process." The sinologist, James Legge, translates. "I seek a unity all-pervading." When Pound translates the same passage he sees within the Chinese characters representations of a string passing through holes in a coin, and of earth, stem and leaf. He crams in everything he sees within the four ideograms of Confucius's remark:

I one, through, string-together, sprout (*that is*: unite, flow through, connect, put forth leaf). For me there is one thing that flows through, holds things together, germinates.   (*Confucius* 263)

In "I cannot make it flow thru," the old poet admits that even as he has failed to "write Paradise," so, too, his restless, irritable self has not become authentically the Confucian sage.

Fenollosa: the luminous ideogram

The cryptic concluding line of Canto 89 — "or, if you like, Reck, at Lake Biwa" — is one of the odder references in the *Cantos*, for within it there is buried a figure whose name goes unmentioned in the poem, but who is everywhere present within it. In the grounds of a temple near Kyoto, overlooking Lake Biwa, Michael Reck, a young friend of the poet's, had made a visit of homage to the grave of Ernest Fenollosa. Certainly Pound did not wish to obscure a debt: the *Cathay* translations of 1915 were "from the notes of the late Ernest Fenollosa"; in the *Noh* translations of 1916–17 he rightly gave Fenollosa's name precedence over his own. He edited, annotated, published, tried to keep in print, and urged everyone to read Fenollosa's seminal essay, "The Chinese Written Character as a Medium for Poetry."

Ernest Fenollosa studied philosophy at Harvard, and in 1878, during a period of aggressive westernizing in Japan, was appointed professor of philosophy at Tokyo University. An authority on and preserver of Japanese culture, he was appointed Imperial Commissioner of Fine Arts in 1886. From 1896 to 1901, he concentrated on the study of Chinese poetry, working with Japanese instructors. (In dealing with all texts, Pound likes to leave traces of cultural transmission: his approach to China through Fenollosa and Japan explains why, in the *Cantos*, Chinese names and words, such as Sō-Gyoku and the four-line poem in Canto 49, often appear in Japanese forms.) Fenollosa died suddenly while on a visit to London in 1908, within a few days of Pound's arrival from Venice. By 1913 Pound, who had already shown some interest in Chinese poetry, had met Fenollosa's widow and become enthusiastic about her husband's work. Knowing that Fenollosa's unorthodox views might find a more productive reception with a poet than with scholars, she sent Pound the manuscripts and notebooks on Chinese and Japanese literature.

In many ways Pound's interests in the language and procedures of poetry, as well as in relations between poetry and "reality," had been developing in parallel with Fenollosa's, who practiced, as did Pound, ambitious cultural syncretisms that enjoyed taking ideas from their contexts and recontextualizing them. Fenollosa's vision embraced, among other things, Emerson, Hegel, esoteric Buddhism and bold analogies among poetry, philosophy, religion and modern theories of science. In his manuscripts Pound discovered a mind much like his own and concepts which, arising from so different a base in experience, acted as confirmation and catalyst. The meeting of east and west through these two minds resulted first in Pound's work on the *Cathay* and *Noh* translations, and had important consequences for the *Cantos* and modern poetics. Quite apart from the many questions of Fenollosa's accuracy in regard to the ideogram, or of the validity of his correspondences between language and the universe, "The Chinese Written Character," which as Pound saw at once is more an *ars poetica* than a study in Chinese philology, retains its writer's sense of excited discovery as well as a fertile suggestiveness (Jacques Derrida cites it in *Of Grammatology*). The story of Pound's understanding of the ideogram, one of error and insight, has been well recounted by scholars, among them Akiko Miyake and Ian Bell. Here we must limit ourselves to brief considerations of two ways in which Fenollosa's thought is present within the language of the *Cantos*: the "ideogrammatic method," and the unorthodox syntax and punctuation.

First, Fenollosa taught Pound how to "read" ideograms (sometimes, as we have seen, with an inventiveness not endorsed by linguists). The Chinese ideogram, as Pound-Fenollosa saw it, is compounded of material pictures which represent actions, "transferences of force." The distinction between noun and verb in western languages, they thought, leads to a misrepresentation of nature, since all events (and this corresponds to Pound's and Fenollosa's understanding of science) are "the meeting points of actions." In the Chinese sign, the eye "sees noun and verb as one: things in motion, motion in things."

Take as a simple example the first ideogram in the *Cantos* (34/171), *hsin*, which Western definition leads towards an abstraction, *sincerity*: 信 The two brushstrokes on the left form the radical, *man*, *human being*. The elements on the right are "word." Thus, the (sincere) man standing by his word. The square figure at the bottom right is the radical for *mouth*, which has words rising from it. Moreover, these words contain energy, they are not inert, as the English "word," but are seen by Pound-Fenollosa as containing *fire*, *flame*. The reader of the *Cantos*, even when unaware of the specific components of ideograms moving within the language, becomes accustomed to this active etymologizing, and recognizes its presence in the English, not always marked by a Chinese sign. An example: "They who are skilled in fire / shall read 旦 tan, the dawn. / Waiving no jot of the arcanum" (91/615). The sun is seen rising above the horizontal stroke of the horizon. Those who have entered the arcanum of this canto, which is filled with images of light, and of light coming forth from a "body of fire," will observe in *tan* more than *dawn*. They will see motion and transfer of force within that sun/fire, and observe the spark that passes between *tan* and the *hsien* ideogram 顯 three pages before (dictionary: "to be manifest"), in which the sun in action produces the "sun's silk" and "tensile" light. A later appearance of *tan* is marked "ONE, ten, eleven" (97/679), which the initiate comes to recognize as Confucian Ode 1.10.11, where fire and dawn are joined, and of which Pound wrote that the *tan* is "engraved in so splendid a fashion that the poetry of three millenia has not equalled it" (Bacigalupo 365). One might suspect even Fenollosa of finding his disciple extravagant, if he had not written, in a theory of meaning perhaps in advance of its time, that a word "means as much as you can see into it, and therefore lights up with a thousand chameleon-like shadings."

The image of a word lighting up is characteristic of

Fenollosa, as he transfers his insights from Chinese poetry into a general theory of language which he expresses with metaphors of light, electricity, illumination. Words are "charged." In that artificial construct, the sentence, "motion leaks everywhere, like electricity from an exposed wire." The original metaphors buried within words "stand as a kind of luminous background." And in a famous formulation Fenollosa writes: "Thus in all poetry a word is like a sun, with its corona and chromosphere; words crowd upon words, and enwrap each other in their luminous envelopes until sentences become clear, continuous light-bands." All of this is reflected in the language of the *Cantos*, a poem which, we recall, begins in the middle of a sentence, ends with an "incomplete" infinitive phrase, and in between is strung together syntactically on an uncountable number of *ands*, weaving that endless sentence (7/24) which, if it were not to distort the interrelated processes of nature, Fenollosa said, "it would take all time to pronounce." Not to labour a point, the reader might learn a great deal about the poem by opening it on any page, and noticing how difficult it is to parse the "continuous light-band" in ways acceptable to the traditional schoolmaster. On such terms, of course, Pound will not pass, for the syntax in both its micro- and its macro-scope expresses Fenollosan "entangled lines of forces as they pulse through things."

In time, Fenollosa's essay became the basis by analogy for what Pound called his ideogrammatic method. We are concerned here less with ultimate theoretical implications of that (non)method, than with ways in which understanding it can help us read the *Cantos*, but also with ways in which foregrounding it too strongly can become a distraction. In his early verse and prose Pound displays what appears to have been a naturally paratactic mode of thought, and this increased with the years. He jumps from one thing to another, places two or more thoughts or particulars next to each other, depends upon the power of gists or aphorisms, and avoids supplying full or coherent explanations. It is not always possible to say where capacity and incapacity begin and end. The result of this (in)capacity, however, is a vigour of style and the possibility of an immediate participation by the reader in helping to create meaning. Moreover, that meaning usually "sticks" much more than it would if supplied by the poet as "exposition." In latter years, Poundian discourse, with its leaps of thought and its refusal to identify allusions, became so elliptic that, in an otherwise warm message, Wyndham Lewis burst out, probably with calculated therapeutic intent, "Your last letter undecipherable, just cannot imagine what lies beneath the words. Have you anything really to say?" (*PL* 289). Certainly, after all the indulgences we grant to poetry, Pound's late letters cast shadows of doubt over parts of the later cantos, especially passages in *Thrones*.

Ronald Bush has argued that the ideogrammic method *per se* did not consciously provide the procedure for the *Cantos* in its early stages. Nevertheless, it is possible to see aspects of the method − juxtaposition without explanation, forming "new wholes" − in Pound's pre-*Cantos* poetics of condensation and concentration, as in the famous two-line Imagist poem, "In a Station of the Metro." Pound was acutely aware of the conflict between an ambition to write an epic or very long poem and a dedication to extreme concentration of image and vortex, with their aesthetic of epiphany or sudden revelation. In 1920, struggling to find a form or method for the *Cantos*, he was working out the fusion of the supple, inclusive Jamesian sentence and the concentration of the Fenollosan-Chinese "transference of forces." He wondered, in a two-page long comic non-sentence in the style of James, whether "the sentence being the mirror of man's mind, and we having long since passed the stage when 'man sees horse' or 'farmer sows rice', can in simple ideographic record be said to display anything remotely resembling our subjectivity" (*PD* 3). This is not a rejection of Fenollosa by any means, but rather a recognition that *simple* adaptations of the methods of Chinese poetry are neither possible in English nor sufficiently elastic for the materials he might wish to include in the long poem.

At times it becomes convenient to talk about a number of lines, or a canto, or a group of cantos, as "an ideogram," but this really leads to imprecision. For one thing it is difficult to continue the statement by saying what it or they are an ideogram of or for, without coming up with a formulation that is lifeless and unfocused when placed next to the text. For another, there are no frames around these "ideograms," for they immediately ask to be continued outward, to include what comes before and after. There is really no place to halt, to say "here the ideogram ends," unless we are content with the not-very-helpful concept of the entire poem as one large ideogram. The point of the ideogrammic method is to resist easy generalization and Aristotelian logic with facts or a "phalanx of particulars" (74/441). It is important to recognize that "fact" must be understood to include more, say, than that the Renaissance printer, Soncinus, wrote a certain letter to Cesare Borgia on 7 July 1503 (30/148), or that the Bank of the United States was collecting 46 per cent interest in a given year (89/591). Fact must be extended to include tones of voice, the specific language in which thoughts have been written or spoken. It is a fact that a large number of people, through art or philosophy, have testified to a belief, a least, that they have had experiences of "gods" or of the force of divine love or intelligence in the universe; and that they expressed these experiences in often exalted language such as Cavalcanti's canzone in Canto 36, or Erigena's "all things that are, are lights." It is equally a fact that at Pisa in 1945, a guard wanted to "*take* everyone of them g.d.m.f. generals" (74/439) – and that Pound transcribed it in just that way because it is textually more interesting and he knew that in the 1940s such language, spelled out, would cause trouble with publishers. Whatever anyone ever felt, or imagined and left record of, is fact of a sort. In the Poundian text, as Christian Froula has shown, even errors are allowed to remain as facts, for it is the case that someone made them.

Facts or particulars in their specificity, then, offer necessary resistance to the didactic impulse, which is in danger of presenting its "truths" too readily. (The problems and advantages for the *Cantos* of Pound's sense of the relation between

the general and the particular are discussed above [pp. 31–32])
The degree to which Pound knows his truths, has any right
to hold them, or to which they carry conviction, will only be
demonstrated through the arranged thousands of particulars.
In what may be, for the reader, the most helpful of his
remarks on the subject, Pound ignores the nature of the
ideogram and turns to the intended effect:

> The ideogrammic method consists of presenting one facet and then
> another until at some point one gets off the dead and desensitized
> surface of the reader's mind, onto a part that will register.
>
> (*GK* 51)

This is still the Fenollosan transference of forces, if not quite
in a form Fenollosa would recognize. It should be clear, too,
that the inventor of the method recognizes the unpredictabili-
ty of where that "point" may come for any reader at any
given reading.

Ovid: myth, religion the magic moment

Pound made some of his more pithy remarks on his work, as
well as his most damning, as old age and discouragement
forced him to abandon his poem. In an interview with Donald
Hall in early 1960, he told a story that has the ring of the
genteel religious humour of the suburban Presbyterian circles
in which he was raised. A little boy claims to be drawing a picture of God. When an adult tells him that nobody knows
what God looks like, the boy replies, "They will when I get
through." Then, aware that his poem had not attained the
paradiso he had aimed at, Pound added, "That confidence is
no longer attainable." Yet for half a century he had been
drawing his picture of God, inventing a syncretic "religion"
from radical reinterpretations of Graeco-Roman mythology,
the Eleusinian mysteries, gnostic illumination, Christian and
pagan neo-platonism, and other evidences that the human
"tribe," whose tale he was telling, had testified variously to
"the effects of the unknown and of the non-knowable on the
consciousness" (*SP* 50). Pound's religion is in line with a note
Emerson wrote to himself, "Make your own Bible." It is an

extreme of protestant individual authority, and often amounts to Pound's plundering the writings of selected philosophers and theologians for luminous phrases torn from context. If he were "given a free hand with the Saints and Fathers [!]," he thought he might construct a decent philosophy, "something modern man cd. believe" (*GK* 76).

Pound is at his least happy with vague formulations about "the universal religion of all men," or "consciousness of the unity with nature" (*GK* 142; *SP* 59). He is at times reduced to such language in his prose, especially when he is trying to be very clear about the limits of his natural supernaturalism, but he prefers to avoid discourse of the common denominator, anything tending toward, say, Unitarianism or the Perennial Philosophy or Wordsworthian invocations of "faith's transcendent dower." His religious position, in fact, seems close to that of a critic who least abides him, Harold Bloom: that all forms of worship begin in "what you might call the 'psycho-poetry', which is then rigidly codified into a theology. The only vital force, all that allows that theology to be memorable, is the poetry." When gods or intimations of the "undiscussable" paradise appear in the *Cantos*, they come in tatters of the texts through which they were revealed. The opposition between myth and history somewhat breaks down, for myth is not entirely a timeless structure: in the *Cantos* we are constantly reminded of its transformations within time, within history, as it appears, always with some difference, in specific texts or works of art. Aphrodite, Persephone, Odysseus are not "stable" presences, fixed characters or signifiers within the poem. Their tendency to change, both as their textual sources change and as Pound re-contextualizes and re-combines them, presents at times a difficulty for the reader. We are accustomed, that is, to find gods and heroes presented more consistently within a single literary text, as they are usually presented within dictionaries of myth, or in such de-contextualized syntheses as those of Robert Graves and Edith Hamilton.

Thus when Venus-Aphrodite suddenly rises before us at the end of the first canto, she is not allegorized as Love or

Beauty, and many of her "aspects" are missing. It is a highly specific epiphany:

> Venerandam,
> In the Cretan's phrase, with the golden crown, Aphrodite,
> Cypri munimenta sortita est, mirthful, orichalchi, with golden
> Girdles and breast bands, thou with dark eyelids
> Bearing the golden bough of Argicida.

Towards this vivid linguistic showing forth, the goddess, with her adornments of copper (orichalchi) and gold, came from pre-history and the archaic Greek of the Homeric Hymns; gathered to her the Renaissance Latin of a Cretan translator; and now appears or half-appears retranslated in modern English. She is to be worshipped (*venerandam*), and as the Cyprian goddess she rules the high places of Cyprus (*Cypri munimenta sortita est*). In her hand is a golden bough associated with Hermes-Mercury as slayer of Argos (Argicida), which rhymes with the golden bough with which Aeneas entered the underworld, itself a descent that repeats the main subject of Canto 1, Odysseus' descent into the world of the dead. (No literary person of Pound's generation could write or read the words "golden bough" without thinking of Frazer's *Golden Bough* and the impact of those nineteenth-century inventions, the Science of Religion and Comparative Religion.) Aphrodite reappears throughout the poem in all her names and moods, sometimes clearly herself, sometimes merging with other goddesses. Like Whitman's "illustrious émigré," she passes through many cultures and languages, to arrive at the present. Here she is in the Pisan cantos, a rather different Aphrodite from that of Canto 1: as the mother of Aeneas, as a memory of the poet's own love, Olga Rudge, and as the beautiful central figure in Manet's "Bar at the Folies Bergère":

> Manet painted the bar at La Cigale or at Les Folies in that year
>   she did her hair in small ringlets, à la 1880 it might have been
> red, and the dress she wore Drecol or Lanvin
>   a great goddess, Aeneas knew her forthwith   (74/435)

The first four cantos are dominated by tales from classical mythology; after that one cannot read many pages without encountering gods, although they are sometimes disguised. Not all of these tales or rites are from the *Metamorphoses*, but Ovid is a convenient representative figure for a consideration of myth and religion in the *Cantos*. We have seen that on one occasion, under questioning by Eliot, Pound said that he believed in the Confucian *Great Digest*. (It was a serious answer, but must be understood, too, as rhetoric designed to throw Eliot's Christian terms of discussion off balance.) In fact, neither Pound's restless temperament nor his poetic would be contained by Confucian balance and modesty of aim. So in one of the key phrases in the *Cantos* we read that the poem takes place between two dynamic centres of wisdom, each supplementing the other, "Between KUNG and ELEUSIS" (52/258). We will return to the Eleusinian mysteries, but the polarity Kung/Eleusis is also indicated as Kung/Ovid. We can observe the close connection between Ovidian myth and Eleusinian ecstasy in a "Credo" of 1930 (*SP* 53). There, in another riposte to Eliot's question, he writes that he has "for a number of years answered such questions by telling the enquirer to read Confucius and Ovid." Myth goes into action, for he would, in a desire expressed in the *Cantos* several times, erect a statue of Venus on the cliffs of Terricina and a temple to Artemis in London's Park Lane (where Eliot would be obliged to look at it?). There was a "great treasure of verity" in Ovid and in the subject matter of his long poem (*GK* 299). Yet Ovid, "I keep repeating from one decade to another, is one of the most interesting of all enigmas" (*GK* 272).

The enigma, I take it, is the question of Ovid's "belief." It is also Pound's enigma of himself, the questioning of the rationalist *philosophe* and modern scientist within him of the poet in need of gods. Urbane, sceptical Ovid, whose verse "has the clarity of French scientific prose," let it be known that *Convenit esse deos et ergo esse credemos* — it is convenient to have gods; and therefore we believe that they exist. In the Rome of Augustus and in the twentieth century, "The sceptical age hungers after the definite, after something it can pretend to believe" (*SR* 15). It is easy enough to align

Pound's thoughts on myth and religion, for they address the same problems, with those of at least half the worried writers of the nineteenth century. The interesting difference is in the poetry, where Pound's gods are alive, have a conviction of their own presence, in a way they had not for, say, 2,500 years.

That round figure conveniently takes us back to the pre-Socratic Thales, in whom (through the report of Aristotle) we find an early trace of Pound's image of the magnet forming the rose in the steel dust. Thales, addressing an enigma much like that of Ovid's and Pound's, rejected literal mythological explanations, but posited "soul" pervading the universe, which then allowed him to say that "everything is full of gods." Plato, quoting Thales, speaks of the souls of all things, and so "we shall declare these souls to be gods" (*Laws* 10). The nature of the gods and our relations with them are the subjects of two pieces Pound wrote during the years when he was having the greatest difficulty finding his way with the *Cantos*. "Religio" (1913; *SP* 47–48) is a mock-catechism informing us that gods are eternal states of mind; that we become gods when we enter these states of mind; that there is no harm in thinking of the gods by their names; and that the "hearsay" of their tradition is useful because it "tells us to be ready to look." "Axiomata" (1921: *SP* 49–52) is a curiously uncharacteristic essay in which Pound foregoes his ideogrammic, paratactic style for sequential, numbered statements that attempt to lay out with precison, distinctions and (for him) an almost Wittgensteinian combination of caution and play, what he thinks we may say and not say about the *theos*. There is what he is willing to call an "intimate essence of the universe," about whose nature we are "utterly ignorant," except that we know it is not the product of our own consciousness. To that "essence," following Thales-Plato-Ovid, "there is no reason for not applying the term God, *Theos*." After that, preferences are purely a matter of individual temperament, except in minds that are not free, that are "bound" by tradition. Organized religions are usually "exploitation, control of the masses," and the greatest

tyranny springs from dogma about any transcendent, ir-
reducible unity which imposes its will upon the individual. A
belief − and here we have the Nietzschean tendency in Pound
− is "paralysis or atrophy of the mind."

The gods exist, then, because "no apter metaphor [has]
been found for certain emotional colours" (*GK* 299). It is
"the supreme lie that the splendour of the world is not a true
splendour, that it is not the garment of the gods" (*SP* 431:
401). With such self-issued poetic licence, Pound finds myth
a supple language to think in. His mythological figures are
not, however, exclusively those known to Ovid; the graeco-
roman gods welcome corresponding divinities/metaphors
from all cultures, including some of Pound's invention,
Egyptian Kati, Isis, and Ra-Set, Babylonian Tamuz, Chinese
Kuanon, the Japanese nymph of the Hagoromo, Australian
Wanjina, and the unnamed African seekers of a city of the
mind, Wagadu (both divinity and city), whom we come to
recognize by their cry, "Hooo Fasa." They can metamor-
phose into each other, as they do in Frazer, to become Isis-
Kuanon, Isis-Luna, Circe-Titania, or Adonis-Tamuz.
Weather and landscape are mythologized: winds are person-
fied by their classical names, Zephyrus, the west wind,
Apeliota, the east wind; the dawn star is Eos, the evening star
Hesperus; a mountain near Pisa and another in New Hamp-
shire become a sacred mountain in China, Taishan. Since
humans can become gods to the extent that they partake of
the spirits of the gods or the emotional colours they present,
we find many women as forms or incarnations of Venus-
Aphrodite and Persephone; a mad baroness in New York is
Cassandra; an American soldier is Zeus' ram. The reader
becomes so accustomed to mythological thought that it seems
quite natural that a guard in Pound's prison at Pisa, Mr Edwards, who breaks army regulations to show kindness to the
prisoner, should be an incarnation of Kuanon, the Chinese
goddess of mercy (74/434; 81/519).

Observe a new-born wasp, "green as new grass," emerging
from a nest its mother, whom the poet has been watching
closely, has built from "adobe":

> The infant has descended,
> from mud on the tent roof to Tellus,
> like to like colour he goes amid grass-blades
> greeting them that dwell under XTHONOS
> OI XTHONIOI;   to carry our news
> *eis xthonious*   to them that dwell under the earth,
> begotten of air, that shall sing in the bower
> of Kore,   *Persephoneia*
> and have speech with Tiresias, Thebae   (83/533)

(I have transliterated the Greek. The earth appears in its Roman and Greek forms, Tellus-Xthonos. The Greek in the sixth line is translated by the English that follows. Kore is Persephone.) Two realms communicate with each other, as a close observation of nature becomes a repetition of the action with which the poem began, the descent beneath the earth to speak with the ghost of the Theban prophet, Tiresias. The portentous, epic tone of Canto 1, however, here turns to a friendlier, more intimate movement between two words. It is assumed that the dwellers under the earth will welcome the greeting and news from those still on the earth, brought them by the new-born wasp-messenger. In Canto 1, Hades was a dark, awesome place; here it is governed by its queen, Persephone, with her flowers. In passages such as this, Pound is not "using" mythology, but inventing mythologically. There is no "source," I think, in which Persephone and Tiresias are found together.

Myth, together with the fragments of philosophy Pound is interested in, provides the basis for the *Cantos*' "magic moments." The phrase appears in a letter to his father (11 April 1927) as part of one of the many schemes ("or whatever it is") for the poem. The scheme should not be taken too literally, as the ambivalent "rather like or unlike" indicates, as does the fact that the roman numeral I in the "outline" never arrived at II:

Afraid the whole damn poem is rather obscure . . .
   I. Rather like, or unlike subject and response and counter subject in fugue.
A.A. Live man goes down into world of Dead.
C.B. The 'repeat in history'.

B.C. The 'magic moment' or moment of metamorphosis, bust thru from quotidien into 'divine or permanent world.' Gods, etc.

The poem establishes its magic moments from the start, certainly with the appearance of Aphrodite at the end of Canto 1 and in the encounter with Dionysus in Canto 2:

> When they brought the boy I said:
> "He has a god in him,
>   though I do not know which god."

Canto 4, one of the more complex and marvellous of the cantos, is entirely woven from a series of encounters with mysterious divine energies. We should note, however, that encounters with the gods are by no means always charming or delightful, as indeed they are not in Ovid. Canto 4 is based on classical and Provençal tales of rape, revenge, adultery and murder.

Pound's mythology refuses to rationalize the pre-rational, as Leon Surette reminds us in his study of the mythic, sexual and Eleusinian aspects of the *Cantos*, nor can we always explain "energies gone wrong" (32). Why, for example, in Ovid and in Canto 4, must Actaeon be metamorphosed into a stag, then torn to death by his hounds, in order to appease the wrath of Artemis-Diana, whom he has quite accidentally come across as she is bathing? The gods are "discontinuous" (21/99) within our minds and within the poem. The magic moments often form a "jagged" paradise, "For a flash, / for an hour, / Then agony, / then an hour, / then agony" (92/620). Paradise, we read at 74/438, is not artificial, but is

> spezzato [shattered] apparently,
> it exists only in fragments unexpected excellent sausage,
>   the smell of mint, for example,
>   Ladro [thief] the night cat.

Scotus Erigena: the radiant world

Pound makes little distinction, if any, between myth and religion; nor, within his neo-platonizing, between theology and philosophy; nor, for that matter, among the many "pagan" and Christian neo-platonists who register variations of metaphor, temperament and emphasis within a tradition. Confucianism, myth and a broad neo-platonism based upon images of light, supplement each other throughout the *Cantos*. However, neo-platonism approaches mysticism, which makes Pound nervous, for he sees the dangers of the "inner light," how it can lead away from the social responsibility in the cause of which all his philosophizing and mythologizing is enlisted. The dangers are those of fanaticism and of a selfish concern for individual salvation. The "bestial" fanatic is so convinced of his own truth that he imposes it on his neighbour, defines heresies, reproves those with "courage to live more greatly or more openly" (*GK* 223). Fervour for a "next" world makes one see this one as fallen, secondary, evil, and denies that the splendour of this world is "the garment of the gods" (*SP* 431:*401*). An otherworldly or ascetic Christianity fosters, in Pound's view, the social nihilism he finds as a corollary of Buddhist and Hindu traditions, and leads to a "pie in the sky . . . greed system" (*GK* 79) or to wanting "to bust out of the kosmos" (105/750). There is another mysticism, however, one of which Pound approves, "the ecstatic-beneficent-and-benevolent, contemplation of the divine love, the divine splendour with goodwill towards others" (*GK* 223).

Pound's neo-platonism often approaches pantheism. For John Scotus Erigena, or John the Irishman, one of his favorite philosophers, Nature included all reality: all things that are, are lights, both God and created things. Erigena was a ninth-century scholar whose translations and writings introduced Greek neo-platonism to western Europe. His work brought him into conflict with the Church during his lifetime, and three and a half centuries after his death, Pope Honorius III ordered all copies of his *De Divisione Naturae* be brought to Rome to be burned. This condemnation, of course, makes Erigena all the more attractive to Pound, confirming his belief that platonism in all forms "disturbs people of cautious and orderly mind" (*GK* 45). If Erigena was so dangerous to orthodoxy, he must have touched some corner of verity, must have been part of the "conspiracy of intelligence," a conspiracy into which the reader of the *Cantos* is being inducted. Erigenas tried to maintain his orthodoxy by distinguishing between "Nature which creates" and "Nature which is created," but his work left itself open to the charge of pantheism. His argument, much approved by Pound, that "authority comes from right reason" hardly ingratiated him with the authorities in Rome, but "I suppose he thought himself a good catholic" (*GK* 75).

Erigena's is essentially a negative theology, following that of his master, the early Christian platonist known as Pseudo-Dionysus: all we can say of the source of being is how little we can speak directly of it, how inadequate language is to it. We speak through metaphor, and what we know of God, the Light, or, in Erigena's term, of "Nature that creates and is not created," is *per plura diafana* (100/722), through the many translucent veils of the nature we can see and touch. Pound is a negative theologian in this sense, constantly testifying to the unknowable otherness of the intimate essence. "The mysteries are *not* revealed"; they are beyond prose (*L* 327; *GK* 144).

The essential intuition of neo-platonism is of *nous*, mind, or the divine mind, or Light, which emanates or radiates through all creation, and whose "signatures" we may read. Reading a divine signature was, in fact, what St Hilary was doing as he looked at the oak leaf, in the passage from Canto 92 above (p. 18). Pound, too, reads the signatures, in some of the finest passages in the *Cantos*. In the prison near Pisa he observes minimal traces of nature, including a grasshopper which, with a trace of nostalgia, he sees as the North American katydid. He invokes (in Greek) Gea, the earth goddess, the Great Mother:

> by thy herbs menthe thyme and basilicum,
>> from whom and to whom,
>>> will never be more now than at present
> being given a new green katydid of a Sunday
>> emerald, paler than emerald,
>>> minus its right propeller   (74/435)

As the poem nears its end, he finds himself "saved" from his

own failures not by ideas but "by squirrels and bluejays?"
(116/76)
   Platonists, Pound thought,

have caused man after man to be suddenly conscious of the *nous*,
of mind, apart from any man's individual mind, of the sea
crystalline and enduring, of the bright as it were molten glass that
envelops us, full of light.   (*GK* 44)

Once we have learned to recognize the traces of Pound's
neoplatonic "light-philosophers," we find them present
within such passages as:

> Thus the light rains, thus pours,   *e lo soleills plovil*
>   [and the sun rains]
> The liquid and rushing crystal   (4/15)

In the following passages drawn from the first two pages of
Canto 91, we see the mind moving swiftly away from abstract
reasoning and toward that rapturous imagery of light/water/
crystal/fire that is characteristic of the paradisal moments in
the *Cantos*:

> that the body of light come forth
>   from the body of fire
>
>   . . .
>
> That your eyes come forth from their caves
>   & light then
>   as the holly-leaf
>   qui laborat, orat
>
>   . . .
>
> The GREAT CRYSTAL
>   doubling the pine, and to cloud.
>   pensar di lieis m'es ripaus
> Miss Tudor moved them with galleons
> from deep eye, versus armada
> from the green deep
>   he saw it,
> in the green deep of an eye:
>   Crystal waves weaving together toward the gt/
>   healing
> Light *compenetrans* of the spirits
>
>   . . .

> She has entered the protection of crystal
> > convien chi si mova
> > la mente, amando
> > > XXVI, 34
>
> Light & the flowing crystal
> > never gin in cut glass had such clarity
> That Drake saw the splendour and wreckage
> > in that clarity
> Gods moving in crystal
> > > ichor, amor

For these passages, as always, we need a few glosses, and it is only fair to note that much has been omitted from this invocation of − celebration of − some "Reina," a composite queen who includes Aphrodite, Elizabeth I and an androgynous Egyptian divinity of Pound's invention, the Princess Ra-Set. Yet such assured writing can only spring from some profound "belief" in the rationale for myth that we have been discussing. It is "symbolist" poetry, in spite of Pound's lifelong distancing of himself from Symbolism, which he associates with a softness and blurring of effects. The aesthetic-religious program behind such lines is expressed in an essay of 1928 (note the neo-platonizing in the "radiant world" and the Fenollosan "moving energies"):

We appear to have lost the radiant world where one thought cuts through another with clean edge, a world of moving energies . . . magnetisms that take form, that are seen, or that border the visible, the matter of Dante's *paradiso*, the glass under water . . . these realities perceptible to the sense, interacting . . .   (*LE* 154)

Glosses: *Qui laborat, orat*, who works, prays; Pound is watchful over his own visionary writing here, for the vision should never take us far from communal obligations. *Pensar di lieis m'es ripaus*, to think of her is my rest; from a Provencal song by Arnaut Daniel. *Compenetrans*, interpenetrating. *Convien*, etc. leads us to *Paradiso* 26.34, where Dante expounds his own light philosophy: All that is not God are *lume*, "beams" of the divine radiance, toward which the mind is moved, in love. *Ichor* is the ethereal fluid in the veins of the gods and, in apposition with *amor*, love, suggests that love infuses the universe in the manner of this imagery of flowing crystal light. Few writers in the twentieth century have afforded such sustained sublimity, and Pound characteristically prevents it from becoming intolerably sublime with "gt/", a reminder that this is being written, typed; by the American familiarity of 'Miss Tudor" and by the surprising "gin."

Scotus Erigena is joined in the poem by other neo-platonists. Grosseteste is present through several citations of *lux enim*, which derives from his "For light of its very nature diffuses itself in every direction" (see *LE* 160–61). The tag appears, for example, in an anguished lyrical passage at 110/781:

> Falling spiders and scorpions,
> Give light aganst falling poison,
> A wind of darkness hurls against forest
> > the candle flickers
> > > is faint
> Lux enim –
> > versus this tempest.

Richard of St Victor (twelfth century), theorist of the degrees of love, in whom Pound had been interested from his youth, provides the Latin epigraph for Canto 90, which Pound translates as: "The human soul is not love, but love flowing from it . . . it cannot, ergo, delight in itself, but only in the love flowing from it." Plotinus (third century) is the guide who leads the poet out of hell in Canto 15. He returns from time to time in the poem, making a major reappearance in *Thrones*, with rather too much of his Greek (untranslated, and badly transcribed, at that).

What is remarkable is the fusion Pound achieves among his classical, Confucian and neo-platonic texts. Each of the three retains its character while finding itself drawn into fields of force by the others, either by ideogrammic juxtaposition or linguistic fusion. Richard's "There is a certain fire within us" is set next to Ovid's "There is a god within us, by his moving we are warmed" (*SP* 72:74). A cluster of images at 95/644 provides a fine example of Pound's syncretism: it begins with a prayer to the Queen of Heaven; moves to the Ovidian goddess, Leucothea, metamorphosed into a seagull, who brings neo-platonic light shining *per diafana*, through seen things that transmit and reveal it; then to images of crystal waves and solid light that frame three ideograms from the Confucian *Ta Hio*, which Pound translates as "near to benevolence." Pound's Confucianized platonism, or platonized Confucianism, provides many of the most beautiful, inventive and convincing passages in the poem.

Cavalcanti: intelligence of love

By now, the reader may feel bewildered by Pound's extraordinary in-gathering of texts and traditions, including Homeric and Ovidian myth, Confucian ethics, and neo-platonic Light. That bewilderment, however, is part of the poem's assault upon our received sense of history and values. The *Cantos* invites us to enter a powerful counter-history, one radically opposed to the dominant order of the modern world, including the "logic" and "reason" that support it. Pound was aware that his method could be read as an "aimless picking up of tidbits," but those tidbits, he hoped, would cohere under the pressure of a "definite intention," a direction of the will (*SR* 8). Although the splendours of paradise are ineffable and cannot be fittingly narrated nor even remembered, "Nevertheless by naming over all the most beautiful things we know we may draw back upon the mind some vestige of the heavenly splendour" (*SR* 96).

For reading the poem, it is wiser to accept Pound's revisionary history as a "naming over," as a search for "the exalted moment" (*SR* 97), rather than as an account of what (really) happened. One line of his secret history – repressed, he believed, by the usocracy and the Church because of its potentially disruptive powers – begins with the Greek Eleusinian mysteries and leads forward to the thirteenth-century poet, Guido Cavalcanti. A translation of Cavalacanti's "philosophical canzone," *Donna mi prega*, (A lady asks me), is one of the great set-pieces of the poem (Canto 36). We will put aside the question to what extent Pound's history here is verifiable or is an inspired guess. What is important is the sense conveyed that there are *other traditions* available to us, traditions suppressed or forgotten, which will not support our age's dominant politics or its construction of "reality." A succinct statement of the buried history we are concerned with here came in Pound's "Credo" of 1930: "I believe that a light from Eleusis persisted throughout the middle ages and set beauty in the song of Provence and of Italy" (*SP* 53). Let us follow that light within the *Cantos*.

We have already noted the important line, "Between KUNG and ELEUSIS" (52/258), where Kung/Confucius leads us towards reason and ethics, Eleusis towards sacred mysteries. The polarity may also be taken to indicate the rational or Enlightenment side of Pound's mind and the irrational or pre-rational, the kind of knowledge or consciousness that lies beyond "the vain locus of verbal exchanges" (*SP* 57). We may think of the *Cantos* as a field of force in which we and the poet are "between" these two poles – rational/irrational – not as torn between irreconcilable opposites, but as attempting to achieve some harmony or reintegration of them. Within the *Cantos* Pound seeks his unity by quick juxtapositions, combined with an exchange of vocabularies among texts. It is perhaps as if by forging a reality *of* language, the poem will suggest a reality beyond language. We are following the light from Eleusis, although Eleusis is not mentioned in the following brief exchange which begins in Latin and ends in Cavalcanti's Italian:

> Ut animum nostrum purget, Confucius ait, dirigatque
> ad lumen rationis
> perpetuale effecto/   (59/324)

Here Pound is quoting from a Latin commentary on Confucius by an eighteenth-century French Jesuit. The meaning of the Latin is: "So that we may purge our minds, Confucius said, and direct [or guide] them to the light of reason." Then a quick cut to a phrase from Cavalcanti's canzone, literally "perpetual effect," which is translated in Canto 36 as "[Love] shineth out / Himself his own effect unendingly." That shining out of Love is an emanation of the neo-platonic light, or, in Pound's translation, "the white light that is allness" (36/179). Thus two metaphors, as it were, employing the same word or concept, "light," are made to conjoin or modify each other: the light of Reason meets with the light of

Love. And the Greek Eleusinian light is present through Cavalcanti because – because Pound believes it is.

It should be noted that the occult history Pound develops is, in broader outline, by no means idiosyncratic or original with him. There is a great deal of scholarly debate on its components and their relations with each other – the exact nature and meaning of the cult of Eleusis; the ways in which the Eleusinian and other mystery religions and the pagan gods took on subterranean existence through the early Christian centuries and middle ages; the influence of older and much-intermixed eastern traditions upon the Cathar religion which threatened to dominate southern France in the twelfth and thirteenth centuries, until suppressed by the Albigensian crusade and the Inquisition; the presence of all this within the vogue of courtly love and the troubador song associated with it; and the refinement of that tradition in the "heretical" verse of Cavalcanti, which brings together precisions of philosophical terminology, neo-platonic religious sensibility, sexuality and the sacred, through an *intelletto d'amore*, intelligence of love. The complexity of the tradition Pound is in part writing within, in part inventing, grows ever greater as he reaches out to include within it Scotus Erigena, Dante, and countless others. We want something like a clear statement of the meaning of all this within the poem; perhaps the clearest such statement is one the poet translated, with approval, from an Italian popular history:

Paganism, which at the base of its cosmogonic philosophy set the sexual phenomena whereby Life perpetuates itself mysteriously throughout the universe, not only did not disdain the erotic factor in its religious institutions but celebrated and exalted it, precisely because it encountered in it the marvellous vital principle infused by invisible Divinity into manifest nature.   (*SP* 55)

This is what, in the essay on Cavalcanti, Pound thinks of as a Mediterranean sanity, which avoids fanaticism and asceticism (*LE* 154).

At Eleusis, not far from Athens, an annual ceremony celebrated the rites of Demeter, the grain-goddess, and her daughter, Persephone, whose yearly return from the underworld marks the return of spring and the growth of new crops. In one element of the ceremony, priest and priestess re-enacted the archetypal planting of seed in the Earth-mother by the male rain-god. Pound, as had his generation, learned to read the myth and ceremony through Frazer's *Golden Bough*, which suggested a symbolic connection between human sexuality and the fertility of nature. Scholars have debated whether or not the "sacred marriage" included copulation or only ritual re-enactment; Pound preferred the more literal interpretation. In a gloss on the final lines of Canto 45 —

> Usura slayeth the child in the womb
> It stayeth the young man's courting
> It hath brought palsey to bed, lyeth
> Between the young bride and her bridegroom
> CONTRA NATURAM
> They have brought whores for Eleusis

— he wrote that "Eleusis is *very* elliptical. It means that in place of the sacramental ------- in the Mysteries, you 'ave the 4 and six-penny 'ore. As you see, the moral bearing is very high, and the degradation of the sacrament (which is the coition and *not* going to a fatbuttocked priest or registry office) has been completely debased by Xtianity, or misunderstanding of that Ersatz religion" (*L* 303). The mysteries of death and rebirth, of vegetation, and of a light as phallic seed entering the dark cave where the sacred marriage is enacted, then the reappearance of Persephone, are recreated in the lyrical-erotic-anthropological Canto 47:

> The light has entered the cave. Io! Io!
> The light has gone down into the cave,
> Splendour on splendour!
> By prong have I entered these hills:
> That the grass grow from my body,
> That I hear the roots speaking together,
> The air is new on my leaf

Against a culture dominated by "sadistic and masochistic" tendencies in the Church, then, "some non-Christian and inextinguishable source of beauty persisted throughout the Middle Ages maintaining song in Provence" (*SP* 58).

"*Donna mi prega*," then, as translated in Canto 36 and glossed extensively in the essay on Cavalcanti (*LE* 149–200), leads to an idealized, spiritualized eroticism within which intelligence, sex, love and the fertility of nature are reunited. The poem attempts to create a sensibility opposed to an eroticism of immediate gratification, hedonistic, commercialized, and symptomatic of the *ethos* of the "usurocracy," of a culture controlled by unrestrained enterprise finance. Following the Cavalcanti translation, we hear an ecstatic "Sacrum, sacrum, illuminatio coitu" ("Sacred, sacred, illumination in coitus"), clearly contrasting with those "whores" brought in to replace the sacred mysteries of Eleusis.

The erotic, then, is associated in the *Cantos* with divine Love in the universe, with the "natural" and with fertility. In Canto 36 that Love is said to derive from a "seen form," to take its state in memories of all beautiful or fine things, and to become "Custom of the soul / will from the heart." It should lead towards social action. The light from Eleusinian mysteries, as it passes through Cavalcantian Love, brings us to a subject that may seem far from sacred, economics. Poundian economics, however, is a realm in which, to quote a sentence the poet discovered in Richard of St Victor, "The plenitude of law is charity" (*SP* 71:*73*).

Douglas: money

Canto 38 begins with two lines from Dante's *Paradiso* about the evil of falsifying money, then settles into three pages of a lively babel of post-war voices discussing international skulduggery of munitions salesmen and the financial manipulations of those who "faire passer ces affaires / avant ceux de la nation" (put their business before that of the nation). Suddenly we hear the patient, plodding voice of Major C. H. Douglas expounding his $A + B$ Theorem, the central insight behind his radical Social Credit proposals. Douglas, an engineer, studying the books of firms he worked for, had decided that under the present system purchasing power could never catch up with prices (which include bank charges), thus producing a "clog" in the system and the evils that spring from scarcity economics. Douglas is urged on by exasperated American interruptions: "any damn factory," "damn blast your intellex." Then, just before we return to our modern hell and hear the munitions maker, Krupp, declare that "guns are a merchandise," we are transported swiftly, if briefly, to a moment of Dantesque illumination:

> and the light became so bright and so blindin'
> in this layer of paradise
> that the mind of man was bewildered.

That moment records Pound's encounter with Douglas in 1919, which led to a lifetime of economic investigation and pamphleteering, and, eventually, to the prison cage at Pisa and thirteen years in an insane asylum.

For the long-projected epic poem, which he was having trouble formulating, Douglasite moral-libertarian economics provided a vital link between past and present. That is, to the extent that the poem was to be an epic it must include history, and "only a sap-head can now think he knows any history until he understands economics" (*LE* 86). More important, economics transforms what might have been an eclectic rummaging through the classics into an ever-present concern with how history might inform us where we are and how we got here, how we might make sense of the world, and toward what goals we might at least dream of moving. If one feels the need of *directio voluntatis*, direction of the will, one must have a direction *for* the will. Some of the money-in-history passages in *The Cantos* may be miscalculated as material for poetry, yet we might pause to wonder how slack this poem might be without its economic thrust. Putting aside the question how practical or accurate might be Pound's Douglasite economics (which he modified with ideas drawn from other monetary theorists such as Silvio Gesell, the inventor of "stamp scrip" or "timed money"), I would argue that economics as the focus of "ideas into action" is what rescues the poet from being, as Wyndham Lewis charged him, a man in love with the past. The feeling of the poem is fired not only by a search for the Good and the Beautiful, but, as Pound wrote of Gesell, by "a detection of injustice coupled by a passion for justice" (*SP* 274:*244*) and an awareness of "murder by capital" (*SP* 277:*197*). The study of money transformed the poem and returned it to a lost tradition: Shakespeare and Dante had mentioned "the subject,"

> and the lit profs discuss other passages
> > in abuleia
> or in total unconsciousness   (93/627)

(For *abuleia*, paralysis of the will, as a constant in history, see also 5/19 [the Renaissance] and 54/285 [seventh-century China].)

It may seem an abrupt change of direction, and it is often abrupt within the poem, to move from a world of myth, sacred mysteries, and Cavalcanti's inspiring Love to a consideration of money and economic policy, but we are reading a poem which insists upon "No dichotomy" (87/575). The ideal city the poem asks us to imagine and build must be founded upon harmony with nature, the Confucian "Process," which in combination with our labour, inventiveness and heritage of civilizing skills, should provide an abundance of things we need for a decent life, including time for leisure, time not palsied with economic anxiety. Pound believed, with the technocrats of his generation, that the problem of production had been solved; it followed that the political problem was to see that "the abundance is divided in just and adequate parts among all men" (*GK* 157). This happy approach to a civic paradise, however, is thwarted everywhere by *Usura*, the personfication of the grab-at-once mentality, the power of hogging the harvest, and more importantly of the monetary assumptions and systems through which Usura's thriving servants profit at the expense of most people.

A usurious system founds its exorbitant profits upon negation, the creation or illusion of scarcities; upon the diversion of our desires into the production and consumption of things we do not need (most damagingly, the machinery of war); and upon convincing us that money, which should be only a useful sign, free from private control and regulated for the welfare of the "whole people," is also a commodity in short supply. It is a commodity, moreover, which financiers have obtained license to create for themselves *ex nihil*, from nothing (46/233–34). The problem is not *per se* that some men are richer than others, but in the systems and false mythologies through which they maintain their advantages,

> "and having got 'em (advantages, privilege)
> there is nothing, italics *nothing*, they will not do
> to retain 'em"   (77/464)

We observe sexless Usura's progress (for, although personified, Usura is an "it") in the medievalized Canto 45, both a dance of the dead and a chant of exorcism, in which it blights our housing, food, art, crafts and marriages, and provides a perverse banquet for the dead, while the living go hungry:

> with usura, sin against nature,
> is thy bread ever more of stale rags
> is thy bread dry as paper,
> with no mountain wheat, no strong flour.

So the language of Pound's economic writings, even as they aim at a "scientific" lucidity, are filled with the language of religious discourse, as he denounces the worship of the golden calf. The nineteenth century, when usury came conclusively to power, created "a species of monetary Black Mass" (*SP* 346:*316*). Against a Jeffersonian concept of credit based on the dogma that "The earth belongs to the living," we find a dead hand ruling by the "superstitious sacrosancticity of " 'property' " (*SP* 256:*226*). It is unfortunate that Pound misread Marx, whom he accused of endowing money with properties of a quasi-religious nature, for Marx, especially in his early writings, sounds at times quite Poundian and employs many of the same arguments and metaphors (the financier as "alchemist," for one). For Marx, too, money had been perverted into a "visible divinity – the transformation of all human and natural properties into their contraries," and the dichotomy between ethics and economics was fatal: If I ask the political economist, Marx wrote in the economic manuscripts of 1844, if I should follow economic laws by offering my body for sale or selling my friend into slavery,

then the political economist replies to me: You do not transgress my laws, but see what Cousin Ethics and Cousin Religion have to say about it . . . It stems from the very nature of estrangement that each sphere applies to me a different and opposite yardstick — ethics one and political economy another.

There is no space here for a consideration of the important differences between the optimistic amateur, Pound, and the more thorough economic philosopher, Marx. Pound, whose economic thought ceased to develop in the 1930s, had no access to those early writings of Marx for which he would have had most sympathy. He is clearly puzzled by Marx and Lenin, quoting them with approval when possible: there are extensive quotations from *Capital* in Canto 33, and approving glances at Lenin (74/429; 100/713). But like other writers of his time, Pound was unable to disentangle Marx's thought from Soviet and Stalinist doctrine and practice. Yet his central distinction is the Marxist one, between use-value and commodity-value. As an optimistic man of good will speaking to other men of good will, he was at his most disarmingly rational when he thought, in Eliot's *Criterion* in 1935, that if he could make a few points to a gathering consisting of Marx, Lenin, Thomas Aquinas and Scotus Erigena, they would accept his statements "almost instantly" (*SP* 282:*252*). On one concept Pound and Marx agree, that "Money is not a product of nature but an invention of man" and that "what man has made he can unmake" (*SP* 346–47:*316–17*). Although an enlightened and radical view of monetary policy seemed to him the pivot around which a humane society might move with maximum individual liberties, few would listen to his Douglasite solutions to the world's evils. Few readers have found the *Cantos*' technical (as opposed to prophetic) considerations of money inspiring. Pound's frustration increased. "I know of no subject," he wrote in his *ABC of Economics* in 1933, "in which it is harder to arouse any interest whatsoever." The words of the Sinn Fein leader, Arthur Griffith, are a refrain throughout the poem:

                              Perfectly true,
"But it's a question of feeling,
"Can't move 'em with a cold thing, like economics."
                         (19/85; also 78/481; 97/678)

At 103/735 Griffith's words are followed by an ironic "ut delectet," i.e., that poetry should please, not instruct in economics or attempt to move us toward action based on inferences from the dismal science. Yet pleasing is not to be split from teaching and moving. To that end, much of the poem dramatizes an epic struggle between forces of light and darkness over the control and definition of money.

We must concern ourselves with observing that struggle within *The Cantos* rather than attempting a thorough explanation of Pound's ideas, which the interested reader can better pursue in the economic pamphlets gathered in *Selected Prose* and in Earle Davis's clear exposition in *Vision Fugitive*. It will be helpful, however, to make distinctions among three aspects of Pound as purveyor of economic wisdom: (1) The Old Testament prophet, denouncing evil with searing rhetoric, urging us into paths of righteousness and towards the City of God; (2) The prosecuting attorney and investigatory journalist, unveiling the iniquities of bankers and their bought politicians; and (3) the technical historian, studying in often maddening detail the significance of coinage and interest rates in history.

Pound as prophet links himself directly with the prophets of the Old Testament, in particular Leviticus 19, where God instructs the people in economic justice: "The wages of a hired servant shall not remain with you all night until the morning" (which might be read as a version of the $A + B$ Theorem), and "You shall do no wrong . . . in measures of length or weight or quantity," which Pound connects with the financiers' power to manipulate money as a standard.

    and there is no need for Xtns to pretend that
        they wrote Leviticus
        chapter XIX in particular
            with justice Zion   (76/454)

To which is appended the question, "Why not rebuild it?" —

that is, Zion as the city of God. The great prophetic set-pieces of the poem are Canto 45 and the scatological "Hell cantos" 14 and 15, modelled on Dante, whose "whole hell reeks with money . . . Deep hell is reached via Geryon (fraud) . . . and for ten cantos thereafter the damned are all of them damned for money" (*LE* 211). The Hell cantos present a revolting and savage comic book landscape stripped of all possibility of natural increase; its profiteers and financiers are anonymous, for "only the last letters of their names [have] resisted corruption" (*L* 293). There they mingle with their hangers-on, among them bought journalists and academics, and conservatives "distinguished by gaiters of slum-flesh." Unlike the damned of the *Inferno*, the denizens of Pound's hell appear unaware of their surroundings or that they are supposed to be suffering. We may see this oozing "last cess-pool of the universe" as horrid, but for them it is merely an image of their states of mind in life: it has become "natural" to them. If they howl, it is not in spiritual anguish, but because they cannot stain jewels in their mud. "THE PERSONNEL CHANGES," but Usura's dread corporation goes on.

In his prophetic role, Pound continues both a British tradition of moral-economic reformers that would include Cobbett, Morris and Ruskin; and an American tradition of Populist anti-bank, anti-gold-standard politicians, such as William Jennings Bryan ("You cannot crucify mankind upon a cross of gold"). Pound refuses to stop with denunciations and a wringing of hands. He drove himself − and drives us, too, if we are to read his poem − into prolonged, technical, even boring, *work*, so that his and our protests against "the system," and our efforts to construct a better system, might be grounded upon solid evidence and clear distinctions. Otherwise, we will remain at the level of the "lit profs" or the parlour liberals for whom he had such contempt. The more rebarbative passages on coinage and interest rates −

> AND in 1859 a dirhem "A.H. 40" was
> paid into the post-office, Stamboul.
> Struck at Bassora
> 36.13 English grains . . .

. . .

                    Andoleon of Paeonia,
        Gold scrupulum: 20 aces. A.U. 437
                                   (97/668–69)

— function as indications of the detailed study the poet thinks
necessary. They may be inaccurate, yet to say that in matters
of history, economic or otherwise, Pound or the sources in
which he placed enthusiastic faith were sometimes wrong, is
not always to deny the justice of the larger argument. Alexander Hamilton, in terms of economic policies, allowing
some poetic hyperbole, probably was "the Prime snot in ALL
American history" (62/350). If we hold back from accepting
that view (indeed, no successful banker could accept it),
Pound's larger point is that few of us will take the trouble to
study Hamilton's policies in detail, or to apply such studies
to our present state of affairs. The passage just above is intended to stimulate our curiosity and to demonstrate that the
prophet-poet has done his homework, that he is something
more than rhetorician and radical moralist.

Important results of Pound's research are dramatized in
Cantos 42–43, about the triumphal founding of the Monte dei
Paschi, a seventeenth-century Sienese bank. "Two kinds of
banks have existed: The MONTE DEI PASCHI and the
devils" (SP 270:240). For banks per se are not evil; they are
useful, necessary, and they can be founded on principles of
sharing rather than usury, upon the abundance of nature, and
on the credit of the whole people, bypassing private banking
and exercising their powers through a benevolent government's right of sovereignty over money. It was "to restart the
life and production of Siena, that this bank was contrived,"
through a Douglasite adequacy of credit avoiding that "clog
in the system" which is the source of the userer's profit. For
a clear statement of the workings and meaning of the bank of
Siena we must turn to Pound's prose. Yet Donald Davie
reminds us that righteous indignation is worthless if we have
not earned a right to it, and that our "admiration and sympathy for Canto 45 is worthless because it is unscientific
unless we see how the conclusions to be drawn arise

unavoidably from the case in point . . documented from Tuscan history'' (*Poet as Sculptor* 159). That history includes the story of the Bank of Siena and, in Canto 44, additional "documentary" material on the Leopoldine reforms of the later eighteenth century.

In his very old age, Pound wrote, "re USURY: I was out of focus, taking a symptom for a cause. The cause is AVARICE" (*SP* Foreword). "The subject" (economics) and the establishment of social order by appeals to the intelligence of statesman and citizen were more resistant than pamphleteer or poet had counted on through four decades of study and propaganda.

Adams: decline of the republic

With the exception of the thirteen years he was confined in Washington, from 1908 Pound remained in Europe, seldom visiting America. "After the debacle of American culture," he thought, "individuals had to emigrate in order to conserve such fragments of American culture as had survived" (*SP* 161:*131*). He insisted firmly upon his American identity, and dramatised his origins by punctuating the *Cantos* with lingo based on versions of American demotic; "And if your kids don't study, that's your fault. / Tell 'em" (99/705). One of the aims of the poem is to contribute to a re-birth of American "kulchur" and civilisation by returning to forgotten origins, primarily the thought of Jefferson and Adams. Pound's writing is always energized when he feels he is lifting the "historic blackout" without which "they cannot maintain perpetual wars" (89/595). The revisionary drama he makes of American history had always a moral dynamic. He was delighted to find that, as in so many matters, his hero, John Adams, agreed with him;

> IF moral analysis
> be not the purpose of historical writing . . .   (62/346)

By late 1930 Pound was reading that "shrine and monument," the extraordinary correspondence that passed between Jefferson and Adams in their retirement; it was not until later that he was able to obtain the collected papers of Adams. Increasingly, Jefferson's presence in the poem diminishes, although his wisdom continues to be cited, and the livelier language and personality of Adams predominates.

John Adams, leader and theorist of Revolution, first Vice-President and second President, has been presented in American schoolbooks and popular histories as an austere, patrician figure, often contrasted, to his disadvantage, with a more democratic and multi-minded Jefferson. Pound was delighted to discover quite a different Adams from the one most Americans know, a man of passion, curiosity, learning, benevolence and wisdom, one who expressed himself with great variety, pithiness and sardonic vigour. Ten cantos (62–71) are an attempt to make poetry from a collage of language drawn from the writings of Adams, and the "Adams" of these cantos must be seen not only as historical reconstruction, but always as an important *persona* of the poet. Certainly, Adams has never found so warm and lyrical a celebration:

> But for the clearest head in the congress
> > > 1774 and thereafter
> > pater patriae
> the man who at certain points
> > > made us
> at certain points
> > > saved us
> by fairness, honesty and straight moving
> > > > ARRIBA ADAMS (62/350)

The full-throated cry in Spanish is a rebuke to the treatment Adams has generally received, and a rebuke, as well, to the language of Anglo-American politics. In Pound's presentation of a warmer, more passionate Adams, the former president is made to exclaim, at the end of Canto 70, "DUM SPIRO AMO" (While I breathe, I love); and we find next to a quotation from an 1811 Adams letter, the poet's comment:"Beyond civic order: / l'AMOR" (94/634).

Pound's attraction to Adams and Jefferson was essentially two-fold. First, they were a demonstration that one might conceive of political leaders who combine wisdom, benevolence, intelligence and a learning both broad and deep. "From 1760 to 1826 two civilized men lived and to a considerable extent reigned in America". By the latter part of the nineteenth century, however, something like Eliot's "dissociation of sensibility" had entered the public sphere: there was a fatal "division" between "the temper, thickness, richness of the mental life of Henry Adams [John's great-grandson], and Henry James, and that of say U.S. Grant, McKinley, Harding, Coolidge and Hoover." And indeed, at least in British and American politics, as the twentieth century draws to a close, there does appear "a definite opposition between public life" and citizens of learning, culture and sensibility (*SP* 147, 158:*117*, *128*). The main implication of the Adams letters, for the writer of the holistic *Cantos*, was "that they stand for a life not split into bits" (*SP* 152:*122*). More specifically, however, Pound discovered in the writings of Adams and Jefferson statements, which few Americans ever hear, on banks and money, statements which appeared perfectly to support the moral political economy he had developed from the insights of Major Douglas.

Adams especially expressed his opposition to the "swindling banks," which had usurped, with the aid of corrupt politicians, the sovereign powers granted Congress by the Constitution: "To coin money, [and] regulate the value thereof." In spite of his efforts, the new nation suffered under a banking system contrived, as Adams wrote, "to enrich particular individuals at the public expense." The banks had power to create money and credit *ex nihil*, out of nothing, then to loan that money to the nation and its people. With such profitable control over the amount and value of the nation's money, political democracy never found its necessary corollary, economic democracy. "All the perplexities, confusion, and distress in America arise," wrote Adams, in a passage Pound often publicized, "from downright ignorance of coin, credit, and circulation." Yet the power of financial orthodoxy, or of the "Hamiltonian" system, was so strong that Adams's vision in the matter of banking makes him appear a crank – as with wry humor he was aware. The last of the Adams cantos contains a passage which is at once a documentary cutting and a moment of mask or *persona* in which Pound, through Adams's words, comments on his own poem and its inextricable mixture of reason and romance. We are at a point – perfectly indicated by both Adams and Pound in Don Quixote – where to be rational is to appear mad, but where it is mad to accept what the world finds rational or "necessary":

> Funds and banks I
> never approved I abhorred ever our whole banking system
> but an attempt to abolish all funding in the
> present state of the world wd/ be as romantic
> as any adventure in Oberon or Don Quixote.
> Every bank of discount is downright corruption
> taxing the public for private individuals' gain.
>   and if I say this in my will
> the American people wd/ pronounce I died crazy.
>
> (71/416)

Pound emphasizes the last four lines with heavy scoring in the margin.

Seeing his own mind mirrored in that of Adams, Pound gives us an Adams as much like himself as possible. The verse retains Adams's characteristic prose rhythms and diction, but Pound's abrupt cuttings and juxtapositions create a cross-rhythm with Adams's language, designed to remove us from an intelligible, chronological history or autobiography (the two genres are here closely interwoven), and to present an impression or image of Adams's sensibility and unceasingly vigilant activity. It is possible to turn each bit back into conventional history or discourse by locating its origin in the *Works* of Adams. (This labour has largely been done for us in Terrell's *Companion* and in F. K. Sanders' *John Adams Speaking*.) The Adams cantos by their sheer length – eighty pages – push the documentary method begun in the Malatesta cantos to its limit. They are, in that much-misused phrase, "experimental writing," and for most readers they remain an experiment that failed. The Adams–Jefferson correspondence itself is perhaps more interesting, with its dramatic background of political rivals reconciled in old age, and the pathos and unflagging energy of Adams, at the age of seventy-eight, telling Jefferson, "You and I ought not to die before we have explained ourselves to each other."

Adams is not present as an isolated character study, but is woven into the larger text of the *Cantos*. His interest in the Graeco-Roman classics, for example, produces connections with much that has gone before in the poem; as his interest in Justinian's Code and in the *Institutes* of the seventeenth-century jurist, Coke, leads to major treatments of those codifiers of law in later cantos. Through a kind of linguistic fusion, Adams is made to unite, too, with Confucius, Cavalcanti and the author of the *Cantos*. Like Confucius, Adams is minutely concerned with precision of meaning and abuses of words, and wishes (as does Pound) "to show the U.S. the importance of an early attention to language" (78/400). Adams's speech is several times punctuated by the Chinese ideograms which Pound calls "Ching Ming," the sign for "exact terminology." He is, in fact, made as thoroughly as possible a Confucian sage, and one may read these cantos as the *Analects* of Adams. He becomes Cavalcanti, as well, his words interwoven with Italian phrases from *Donna mi prega*:

> foundation of every government in some principle
> or passion of the people
> > *ma che si sente dicho*
> > [but that is felt, I say]   (67/391)

Like Pound, Adams scours history seeking examples of good rulers who lowered interest rates, and of bad governments that made the common man a "mere dupe, as an underworker / a purchaser in trust for some tyrant" (78/395).

The characteristic tone of the Adams cantos is an intermingling of optimism and melancholy, as the speaker reviews the hopes and achievements of the Revolution and the Constitution; recalls the exhilaration of that fresh start for mankind when "few of the human race have had opportunity like this / to make election of government" (77/391); and observes the almost simultaneous onset of the decline of the Republic. American history in the *Cantos* is a field upon which intelligence and civic benevolence must constantly struggle with greed, human frailty and ignorance. There is no space here to discuss all of Pound's revisionary history of the United States, but the outline of that history is quickly sketched at the beginning of his 1937 essay on "The Jefferson–Adams Letters as a Shrine and a Monument," reprinted in *Selected Prose*. From 1760 to 1830, there was an American civilization. This period corresponds roughly with the mature lives of the two presidents. Then, from about 1830 to 1860 the country suffered a period of "mental impoverishment, scission between life of the mind and life of the nation." The years following the Civil War, 1870 to 1930, are a "period of despair." A nation that had bravely begun with leaders such as Adams and Jefferson found itself governed by Hardings, Coolidges and Hoovers. The impoverished Senate of the 1930s contained only "eleven literates" (86/568; *GK* 260); and in 1939 there was an "hysteric [Roosevelt] presiding over it all" (86/568). The spirit of Adams, with his strenuous efforts to maintain peace in opposition to the war party in Congress, is forgotten, his writings unknown under the historic blackout. Usury rules the republic, the Federal Reserve System is its latest instrument, and at the end of Canto 86 the epic poet writes with bitter irony, "Bellum cano perenne" (I sing perpetual war).

Yet in spite of their tragic sense of history, Adams and Pound refused ever to give in to "The wrong way about it: despair" (89/598). Pound's outline of United States history concludes in a present which offers "possibilities of revival" and with the rhetorical question, "should we lose or go on losing our own revolution (of 1776–1830)?" For the poet the odds against our ever seeing the earthly paradise, the state founded upon civic order and moved by Love, were massive, as the *Cantos* exhaustively documents. We will understand a great deal about Pound and his poem (and the John Adams the poem "makes new") if we see them as Confucius is characterized in the *Analects*: "He's the man who knows there's nothing to be done, yet sticks with it (keeps on trying)" (*Confucius* 261).

Mussolini: an excess of emphasis

The *Cantos* is one of the most politically engaged of poems. It is unashamedly idealistic in its aspirations towards peace on earth, civic order, political and economic justice, individual freedom, and a list of qualities and virtues which it is difficult to disagree with, such as responsibility, intelligence, and charity − all of which for Pound are aspects of politics. Whatever we may think of its historical judgements in detail, or of its specific monetary cures for social evils, we will hardly take issue with the poem's attacks on war-mongers, international traffickers in arms, fanatics, obscurers of texts, and all "hoggers of harvest" (88/581) who serve the perverse will of Usura.

Two scandals, however, attend Pound's nobility of purpose: the inclusion in the poem of a simplistic hero-worship of Benito Mussolini and, worse, an unendurable, coarsely expressed anti-semitism. We are on grounds where dispassionate analysis is precluded. As Lyotard has written, following Adorno, anyone who attempts to reflect on historico-political reality today comes up against an abyss marked by certain proper names, among them "Auschwitz." While Pound would never have condoned Auschwitz, nor have thought his writings had even marginally supported it, we may note that in the post-war years, when at last he could not have escaped knowledge of it, he remained silent. Not silent enough, however, as to cease using, in conversation and letters, such expressions as "the jewspapers," nor to refrain from the outburst about "kikery" in Canto 91. There are passages in the poem whereby the poet attempts to detach himself from the *kinds* of anti-semitic discourse that made Auschwitz possible, but they are so oblique − and depend so upon a misguided use of language − as to compound the problem. Only toward the end of his life did he make a clear recantation (in a conversation with Allen Ginsberg): "But the worst mistake I made was that stupid, suburban prejudice of anti-Semitism. All along that spoiled everything." If it came late, at least it came. He never turned against Mussolini.

Much has been written about Pound's anti-semitism and his adherence to Italian fascism. Some writers soften or minimalize the issues; others allow opposition to prevent them finding anything good to say about any aspect of Pound's work. An honourable and understandable position is that of the American critic, Harold Bloom, who simply refuses to have anything to do with Pound. Can we avoid becoming complicit in fascism and anti-semitism by deploring them and their presence in the poem, and by making *ad hoc* separations between form and content? I believe Pound was asking our help in this matter when he said, toward the end of his active life as a writer, "Every man has the right to have his ideas examined one at a time" (*SP* 355:*325*).

During Pound's first years at Rapallo, he showed little interest in Mussolini, the former socialist and journalist who had come to power after his fascist blackshirts marched on Rome in 1922. Pound's at first tentative admiration developed during the 1930s into almost blind hero-worship of the leader who "told his people that poetry is a necessity *to the state*" (*GK* 249). Moreover, Mussolini appeared to have grasped a basic tenet of Social Credit economics when, in a speech of 1934, he declared that the problems of production had been solved and that it only remained to solve the problem of distribution. Pound wrote to his Jewish (and Communist) friend, Louis Zukofsky, "The Boss BURIED scarcity economics ten days ago. NO flowers" (*PZ* xvi). In a tract with the startling title, *Jefferson and/or Mussolini*, Pound argued that the Duce's fascism was right for Italy, but by its very nature – local, *ad hoc*, a continuing revolution dependent upon one man's intuition – not an ideology to be exported. Each nation must find its own way, based upon its own culture and traditions. In one breathtaking sentence, he praises Mussolini, Jefferson and Lenin, all intelligent men of action (*JM* 70). Yet as the curious "and/or" in the title suggests, if Mussolini is modified by seeing him through Jefferson, so does Jefferson become like Mussolini. The American President had "the dynamism of the man who did *get things* DONE" (*JM* 89). Michael Alexander has pointed out that "Pound's return to his American radical roots is obscured for the modern liberal by his simultaneous discovery of Mussolini, whose populist and anti-capitalist side seemed to Pound more significant than his contempt for democratic process" (172).

In *Guide to Kulchur* (1938), we observe quite clearly a fatal reciprocity between aesthetics and politics. Mussolini is here placed in the company of Brancusi, Picabia, Gaudier and Cocteau. He is made to share their artistic genius with his "swiftness of mind," his ability to carry his thought "unhesitant to the root." "By genius I mean an inevitable swiftness and rightness in a given field. The trouvaille. The direct simplicity in seizing the effective means." Brancusi's field is sculpture, Pound's is poetry, Mussolini's the shaping of a nation. The Duce thinks like the author of the *Cantos*, who in turn assembles fragments, *trouvailles*, of the Duce's words and deeds as an ideogram. One is struck by how little Pound seems to know, or to admit to knowing, about Italian fascism in its violent and repressive practice − or in its theory, for that matter. In the *Cantos* the dictator as man who can get things DONE, is praised for turning swamps into fields of grain, supplying water and housing for millions, and dealing severely with conniving profiteers (41/202). He becomes a text read selectively, as Pound reads all texts. Pound was right, at least, to take the Duce seriously, for dangerous as is his inadequate portrait, so was the caricature often supplied by the media, epitomized by Jack Oakie's portrayal in Chaplin's *The Great Dictator* − that of a mere buffoon.

Much of Pound's writing of the 1930s is not only about the ruler, but *for* the ruler. If only he could place his ideas before Mussolini, the Duce would see their rightness! For in spite of its brilliant leader, as late as 1937 Italy's tax system was "still primitive and monetary knowledge rudimentary" (*GK* 242). Mussolini enters the poem on the first page of Canto 41, talking with the poet during their one brief meeting, and bits of that memorable occasion are recalled with starry-eyed lack of irony. The Duce, glancing at a copy of the *Cantos*, finds it "divertente" (enjoyable). Pound does not hear this as the polite remark of a politician, but as evidence of swift insight, Mussolini "catching the point before the aesthetes had got there." A mark of equal genius is the question, "Why do you want to put your ideas in order?", to which the poet replies, "For my poem" (93/626). When the "Boss" is presented with the concept of Gesell's "shrinking money," Pound cannot hear a politician's brush-off: Mussolini "Sd/ one wd/ have to think about that," but unfortunately was hanged "before his thought in proposito [in intention, aim] came into action efficiently" (78/482).

With the collapse of Italy during the war, and the dismissal of Mussolini by the king, Pound's world collapsed. Mussolini, under German protection, formed the pathetic Salò Republic in the North of Italy, which Pound supported in blind hope. He was indeed, as Wyndham Lewis had told him bluntly, "buried alive in a Fascist state" (PL 122), where he continued to find significant fragments in the Duce's speeches:

> "alla" non "della" in il Programma di Verona
> the old hand as stylist still holding its cunning   (78/478)

Note, again, the cult of ruler as artist, master of the precise word. The phrase from Mussolini makes a distinction Pound had long been making, between a right *to* not *of* property.

The Pisan cantos open with Pound in prison and Mussolini, who went out with a "bang, not a whimper," slaughtered in Milan. The hero is now a Christ-like victim, a scapegoat, "twice crucified," once in death, once in his betrayal by his people. Pound had devoted extraordinary labours of propaganda for over a decade toward the "dream" of building the perfect republic, which is figured as "the city of Dioce whose terraces are the colour of stars" (74/425). The Pisan cantos are about putting a shattered world together again, but on new terms, no longer as a reality to be achieved through Mussolini. The poet continues "to dream the Republic" (78/478), and to believe in "the resurrection of Italy," but as a city "in the mind indestructible" and as a matter of pure faith, "quia impossible est" [because it is impossible] (74/442).

At Pisa a strange examination of conscience runs counterpoint to a continued devotion to Mussolini. (There are tears, as well, for others defeated in the war: the L and P, "gli onesti" (the honest ones), at 76/460, are Laval and Petain, leaders of the collaborationist Vichy regime in France.) Where did they — he and the Duce — go wrong? What brought about this failure? There are qualifications and apologies in these cantos, but often so oblique, so cryptic as not readily to be seen. The admission to "losing the law of Chung Ni [Confucius]" in 1945 (77/470) is serious self-incrimination, a recognition of the total loss of Confucian balance in his frenzied behaviour and radio speeches. He had forgotten that

> If a man have not order within him
> He can not spread order about him   (13/59)

He sees himself in Wanjina, from Australian Aboriginal myth, who is also Ouan Jin, "the man with an education," who talked too much, "thereby making clutter," and also has had his mouth removed. Now, from the "death cells," he seems aware that the crazed abuse of language in his wartime broadcasts was far from the "verbum perfectum," the Confucian precise word. As for "poor old Benito" (80/495), neither the Italian people nor most of the fascists around him were worthy of him. Italians are not honest in administration, Pound argued, and, with other faults in the national character, greed and dishonesty brought about the "ruin of 20 years' labour" (77/470). Mussolini's followers were

> all of them so far beneath him
> half-baked and amateur
> or mere scoundrels   (80/495–96)

Was there no fault, then, in the Boss himself? Well, yes, he had come to power through the violence of his paramilitary *squadristi*, but had been unable to control the brutality of his gunmen after the revolution. There had been — as there was in his supporter, the American poet —

> an error or excess of
> emphasis   (80/496)

One must read that as a massive litotes.

In his wartime radio broadcasts, where Pound's anti-semitism was at its most virulent, he claimed that the Axis was defending Europe against a Jewish conspiracy identified, of course, with international financiers. (We should remember that many "polite" people and prominent intellectuals of Pound's generation believed in a Jewish–financial conspiracy. Nor should we forget that this sort of talk is still with us.) In the *Cantos* and in much of his prose, the form of Pound's anti-semitism is based upon a peculiar *code* which in turn depends upon a single, grotesque misuse of language. The irony of this distortion of language is particularly bitter, coming from a writer so concerned for the *mot juste*, the precise definition of terms; it represents that very slippage of language, the "general indefinite wobble" (35/173) which he associates with "jews." To demonstrate the code at length would be both tedious and distasteful, and Pound regretted it in his old age, writing in the Foreword to *Selected Prose*, "In sentences referring to groups or races 'they' should be used with great care." Briefly, the code is: a Jew is not a jew. (Pound often makes the "distinction" with the capital letter.) That is: "jew" is associated with, is perhaps synonymous with, "usurer," but not all Jews are usurers, so they are not jews. Likewise, usurers who are *not* racially or culturally Jews, financiers such as J. P. Morgan and the American "patrician," August Belmont, are in fact "jews." The Rothschilds, favourite target of European anti-semitism, happen to be both. Most Jews, like most non-Jews, are victims of Usura. This line of reasoning lies, for example, behind the first page of Canto 52, where we hear that the sins of "a few big jews," "real jews," cause the anti-semitic prejudice or "vengeance" under which "poor yitts" suffer.

This effort to detach his own brand of anti-semitism from others, and to make room for the fact that there were Jews whom he liked or approved of, brings the condemnation of race prejudice as a "scoundrel's device and usurer's stand-by," a "red herring. The tool of the man defeated intellec-tually, and of the cheap politician" (*GK* 242). Likewise,

"Usurers have no race. . . No orthodox Jew can take usury without sin, as defined in his own scriptures," which is the point of the references to the Old Testament in the *Cantos*. "All racial hates wear down sales resistance on cannon" (*SP* 300:*270*). One cannot claim that Pound was not a racist, for he was, nor did he always adhere to his own "code." But that code allows us to decipher the italicized raving about "kikery" at 91/614. Marx and Freud are not here condemned as Jews, but because their thought was being promoted by the "american beaneries" (i.e., universities), which serve the usurers. If Jacques Maritain and Robert M. Hutchins are associated with "kikery" and "filth," we must remember that one was a leading Catholic philosopher, the other the (non-Jewish) president of a prominent Chicago beanery. And the "treason" of such intellectuals was effectively exposed by a Jew, the French writer, Julien Benda. None of this makes one feel much better about the racial epithets in the *Cantos*. Staring into this abyss, we may agree with Michael Bernstein's precisely qualified generosity in saying that rather than ignore or excuse the poet's fascism and anti-semitism, it is "less demeaning to give him credit for his acts than to remove him from the capacity to err" (117).

Chapter 4

Dissemination

Pound showed little interest in becoming a literary influence in the sense of encouraging poets to sound like him, to employ his mannerisms, or to write poems in imitation of the *Cantos*. (One *Cantos*, like one *Finnegans Wake*, should be sufficient.) He practiced what he preached, the essential doctrine of a literary modernism always making it new, keeping things moving. Thus his highest praise for Zukofsky came in 1954, when the younger poet had finally "got OUT of influence of E.P. and Possum [Eliot]." Zukofsky's earlier work had "more Ez/ in it than I thought," but at last there was no trace of "linguistic parasitism," and "damn all I think yu have got yr/ own idiom" (PZ 208–9). It is hard to imagine Pound enjoying some of the verse for which he has been invoked as an ancestor, especially many of the rambling, "open" American poems of the 1960s and 1970s which recorded, as Daniel Hoffman puts it, what one saw from the window of the bus.

A poet may select ancestors, but not descendants: Pound has had more claimants to his heritage than did Howard Hughes. Beginning in the 1950s and continuing to our day he has been enlisted in skirmishes of the long paleface–redskin wars that run through American literature. Important, overtly tendentious documents in those battles have been the influential anthology of 1960, *The New American Poetry* and its 1982 supplement, *The Postmoderns: The New American Poetry Revised*. Here the palefaces, often associated with Eliot, are poets "in longstanding obeisance to academically sanctioned formalism." The redblooded heroes of the melodrama are those variously called "projectivists, the poetic "underground', the New York School, the Beat Generation, the San Francisco Renaissance, the Black Mountain Poets, or, most generally, the avant-garde." They are the "most truly authentic, indigenous American writers, following in the mainstream of Emerson, Whitman, Pound and Williams." The latest postmodern invocation of Pound as ancestor comes from some of the writers associated with the 1980s pheonomenon, the $L=A=N=G=U=A=G=E$ poets, who combine with an hermetic aestheticism devoted to pure *écriture*, the elimination of the "subject" and an intention of neo-marxist subversion via the avant-garde; in their manifestos and statements of poetics Pound at times finds himself in such odd company as Stein, Althusser, Barthes and Derrida.

Undoubtedly Pound has been an enormous influence upon poetry in English and in many other languages as well. By 1981 his poetry had been translated into twenty-seven languages from, fortuitously, Arabic to Yiddish. Complete versions of the *Cantos* exist in Italian, German and Spanish. There are extensive studies of his impact upon poetry in Romania and Poland. In Nicaragua his association with Italian fascism has not prevented him from being central to the study of poetry under the marxist Sandinista régime. The Nicaraguan Minister of Culture, Father Ernesto Cardenal, who is also an influential poet, acknowledges the unanxious influence of the *Cantos* upon his own verse. His "*Canto Nacional*" is a canto-like mini-epic of Nicaraguan history, juxtaposing images of nature, celebrations of an earthly (marxist) paradise, and indictments of United States banks and imperialism that follow both Pound's documentary style and the scatological, prophetic mode of the Hell cantos. Cardenal's long "Homage to the American Indians" (1970) often looks and sounds like the China cantos.

It is difficult to separate a direct influence of the *Cantos* from all the other means by which Pound's practice and preaching have been disseminated – his Imagist-Vorticist poems and manifestos; approaches to the art of translation; letters both before and after publication; critical essays, especially "How to Read" and *ABC of Reading*; and his untiring efforts as editor of little magazines, anthologist and

encourager and promoter of other writers' work. Often his efforts moved through or in collaboration with others, so it is
impossible to separate direct from indirect influences. Poundian attitudes often came to younger poets through writers
and movements upon which he had been a shaping force, for
example Zukofsky, Oppen and the "objectivist" movement
of the early 1930s; Charles Olson's influential manifesto on
"Projective" verse (1950), which is almost entirely a restate-
ment of Poundian principles; and the practice (and presence
as an American father-figure) of William Carlos Williams.
Dozens, perhaps hundreds of American poets pay tribute to
a conjoined influence of Pound and Williams, often to a line
indicated as Whitman–Pound–Williams, or, in the case of
Robert Duncan, Pound and H.D. For all their individual
achievement, none of the poets through whom Pound exercis-
ed an influence would have written quite as they did without
his example – neither Williams nor H.D., who were among
his earliest friends, nor later Zukofsky, Olson, Ginsberg and
the Robert Lowell of *History* and the *Notebooks*.

A thorough consideration of Pound's impact would abandon traditional concepts of literary influence and work closer
to one Kathryne Lindberg has introduced into Pound studies
(from Deleuze and Guattari), the "rhizomatic." That is,
rather than think on the model of a branching tree, it is more
accurate to think in terms of a "weedlike multiplication of influences and tangled roots." The deepest and more interesting influences, after all, are those which are least ap-
parent and hardest to specify. It is a critical commonplace,
for example, to say that Marianne Moore's often cryptic and
paratactic art of quotation was influenced by Pound and
Eliot. Such a position springs from conditioned ideas about
what is "major" and "minor," and probably from sexist
assumptions as well, for it is arguable that Moore had a
reciprocal impact upon Pound and Eliot. Nathaniel Tarn,
whose work does not particularly look or sound like Pound's,
is more deeply indebted – in the way Pound was to Whitman
– than is, say, Michael McClure, who tells us (remarks not
unlike this might be heard from many American poets of the

1950s to 1970s), "I began to understand [Charles] Parker and [Thelonious] Monk and add them to what I knew of Blake, Yeats, Pound, the Surrealists and the anarchist philosophers."

Remarks by friends of Pound's youth – T. S. Eliot – and of his old age – Hugh MacDiarmid – point in directions where the influence of the *Cantos* is most clear. Eliot thought the poem a treasurehouse of rhythms, cadences, techniques from which younger poets could draw. MacDiarmid emphasized the very point Eliot was avoiding: the value of the *Cantos* in exploring new possibilities for the long poem. Indeed, leafing through collections of twentieth century verse, the reader of the *Cantos* hears familiar cadences. In "The Spoils" (1951), Basil Bunting draws upon the alliterations and rhythms of Canto 1:

> gulped beer of their brewing,
> mocked them marching unguarded to our rear;
> discerned nothing indigenous, never a dwelling
>
> . . .
>
> till we reached readymade villages clamped on cornland

Bunting is at his finest when in his masterpiece, the long poem *Briggflats*, whatever influence remains has gone so deep that we are no longer reminded of Pound. Only a poet who has been listening to the Pisan cantos, and observing their expressive typography and lack of a "normative" line, could write as Lawrence Ferlinghetti in "The Sea and Ourselves at Cape Ann" (1979) (note, too, the Poundian *And*):

> And Creely found his creel
>   yet would not/cd. not
>   speak of the sea
> And Ferrini took the wind's clothes
>   and became the conscience of Gloucester
> Yet none could breathe
>   a soul into the sea
> And I saw the tide pools gasping
>   the sea's mouth roaring
>   polyphoboisterous

None of Pound's inventions has been more abundantly employed by others than his documentary or collage techniques, the pasting in of linguistic "found objects" – spoken utterances, letters, newspaper headlines, bills of lading – in ways that break down a decorum that separates verse from prose. Often, in *Cantos*-like collage poems, what gets pasted in are quotations or borrowings from Pound, as in Robert Duncan's "A Poem Beginning with a Line by Pindar" (1960). An irony of influence is that the *Cantos*, a poem that avoids any consistency of style or diction, often finds one or two of its modes honored as a new decorum.

The *Cantos*, as a long poem breaking with structures of narrative, drama or philosophical discourse (all of which it contains, fragmented), has provided, if not exactly a model, an example or encouragement for many long poems or poetic "sequences," to employ the useful term defined by M. L. Rosenthal and Sally Gall. The most important, and most successful of long poems employing variations on Pound's ideogrammic, documentary and collage methods is William Carlos Williams's *Paterson*, a poem which, like the *Cantos*, remained open, co-extensive with the poet's life, and which ends (although Williams did not publish them as such) in drafts and fragments. In a sense *Paterson* is written against the *Cantos*, aggressively abjuring Pound's cosmopolitanism for the American "local," the history of and present-day life and language in Paterson, New Jersey, near which Williams was born and spent his life as poet and doctor. *Paterson*'s way of beginning *in medias res* is with an initial colon, after which in fragmented or flowing syntax it leaps about in time and between lyrical and documentary modes, incorporating such diverse materials as letters to Williams from Pound and Allen Ginsberg, medical case histories and an entire page of geological data. *Paterson* follows the *Cantos*, too, in a subject where Pound has not been very influential, Social Credit economics. Williams's analysis of American economic history and his denunciation of the Federal Reserve Bank as a "Legalized National Usury System" are straight from Pound. As we might expect, *Paterson* is at its best, and its best is superb, when Williams is most himself, listening and looking in urban New Jersey.

The other long American poem most conspicuously if superficially resembling the *Cantos* — and, equally, *Paterson* — is Charles Olson's *Maximus*, based on the history of his home town, Gloucester, Massachusetts. Olson has warm admirers — and was a friend and teacher who inspired affection — but I have never been able to find more in *Maximus* than a willed application of *Cantos* or *Paterson* methods. I am moved only by the pathos of its worthy but failed ambition. The three poems — *Cantos*, *Paterson* and *Maximus* — and the problematics of the "modern verse epic" have been well studied in Bernstein's *Tale of the Tribe*.

This brief survey of Pound's influence makes no attempt to name all the writers who are indebted closely or indirectly to the *Cantos*. Among British works one should mention MacDiarmid's long *In Memorian James Joyce*, itself part of an even longer, unfinished poem, and David Jones's *The Anathemata*. Interesting and original adaptations in prose of Poundian sensibility and procedures are the brilliant stories in Guy Davenport's *Tatlin!* and *Da Vinci's Bicycle*. One finds traces of Pound in unexpected places, such as the excellent autobiographical poem, a kind of West Indian *Prelude*, Derek Walcott's *Another Life* (1973). In many parts Walcott's long poem, which moves between the lyrical and overlayerings of history and among a great variety of cadences and line-lengths, deftly making collage of documents and speech, is punctuated by multi-lingual, multicultural allusions and quotations. The poem contains two tributes to one of its progenitors. Walcott's "Ityn! Tin! Tin!" reaches back to the tale of Philomela in Ovid through Pound's " 'Tis. 'Tis. Ytis!" in Canto 4. A more direct, less Poundian acknowledgment makes a fitting conclusion to this chapter. Walcott is looking at a picture of Pound in his last years:

> now as I watch
> this twinkling hoar-frost photograph

of the silvery old man bundled, silent, ice-glint
of frozen fire before the enemy,
faites vos hommages

Guide to further reading

In the pages below I note editions I have used, where they are significantly different from the first. For volumes not published in the same year in London and the United States, the earlier date is given.

The *Cantos* has varied from printing to printing, especially in the final pages, which keep changing with publishers' decisions. There is a wide concensus that the best ending for a poem that never ended is the final line of *Drafts and Fragments*, "to be men not destroyers." The most recent printing available to me (New Directions, 1986) creates an unfortunately anti-climactic impression with the addition of the two cantos in Italian and a weak dedicatory fragment. A better text of the poem is needed – perhaps only a complete variorum will do – but the task of preparing it is formidable. The scope of the textual problems is suggested in detail in Christine Froula's *To Write Paradise: Style and Error in Pound's Cantos* (1984) and in Barbara Eastman's *Ezra Pound's Cantos: The Story of the Text*, which gives important variants and has an interesting introduction by Hugh Kenner (1979). Pound gathered his poetry other than cantos in *Personae*, which is almost identical with the Faber *Collected Shorter Poems*, and to which K. K. Ruthven has prepared a *Guide* (1969). There is a *Collected Early Poems* (1976), verse Pound did not reprint, much of which he called "stale cream puffs."

Pound's prose and his translations form a running accompaniment to the *Cantos*. *Guide to Kulchur* (1938; new edition, 1952) is important, and very good reading, as are many of the essays in *Selected Prose* (1973). The early *Spirit of Romance* remains available (1910; new edition, 1952). The more mature *Literary Essays* were edited by T. S. Eliot in 1954. Pound's *ABC of Reading* (1934) is a short, lively introduction to his poetics. I think that of all his books Pound would most want us to know his translations of the three basic Confucian texts collected as *Confucius: The Unwobbling Pivot, The Great Digest, The Analects* (1951). He would also want us to read his edition of Fenollosa's *The Chinese Written Character as a Medium for Poetry* (1919; City Lights Books, n.d.) An especially handy volume, well selected from the poet's critical writings and letters and from early responses to the poetry by others, is J. P. Sullivan's *Ezra Pound: A Critical Anthology* (Penguin, 1970);

unfortunately, it seems to be no longer in print. Of all introductions, the best may be *The Letters of Ezra Pound, 1907–1941*, retitled since 1971, *Selected Letters*, edited by D. D. Paige. New selections from the enormous correspondence continue to appear, including those between Pound and his wife, Dorothy Shakespear Pound, Ford Madox Ford, Wyndham Lewis, and Louis Zukofsky. I find the Zukofsky correspondence the most interesting, although it is often painful, when poetry is not the subject, to observe the poet's increasing disorder and dogmatism of expression from about 1934 on. That disorder extended to crisis in the broadcasts which are collected in *"Ezra Pound Speaking": Speeches of World War II*, ed. Leonard W. Doob (1978).

The indispensible aid for identifying names, dates, quotations and allusions, and for translating all non-English words and Chinese ideograms, is Carroll F. Terrell's monumental labour of love, *A Companion to the Cantos of Ezra Pound* (two volumes, 1980 [C.1–71] and 1984 [C.74–117]), which replaces the pioneering *Annotated Index* of 1957. Terrell often goes beyond basic identification, supplying some of the history, background or Poundian intention behind the allusions. Volume 2 contains an index of proper names and foreign words and phrases in the poem. For each canto there is a list of primary sources, suggested readings in Pound's prose and in related works of history and biography and critical exegeses of the canto. Reading the *Cantos* today, with the *Companion* at one's side, is a somewhat different experience from what it was in former years, when one had to scramble for information about a given passage as best one could among a dozen or more sources. *Caveat lector*: it is not Terrell's fault if we allow his all-too-convenient volumes to prevent us from reading the *Cantos* as poetry, or to deprive ourselves of the pleasure of looking into some of the sources Pound was looking into, such as Homer, Dante, Ovid, Legge's editions of the Confucian texts, the Adams–Jefferson correspondence, Coke's *Institutes*, Catherine Drinker Bowen's biography of Coke and so forth. Our reading of the first two cantos, to take conspicuous examples, is much diminished if we depend only on the *Companion* and other exegeses and do not read Homer's and Ovid's versions of the stories re-told in the cantos. For one thing, we will not have a sense of the differences. One aspect of Pound's didacticism is to stimulate our curiosity, and we should not entirely delegate that to Professor Terrell or the writers of the guides and critical studies mentioned below.

There is a *Concordance* prepared by Robert J. Dilligan *et al.* (1981). Terrell's index gives only proper names and foreign words; the *Concordance* gives *every* word, for example each occurence of "gold" and "eyes," words which might well come to interest one. I find it of great help in tracing linguistic networks and in supplementing a deplorable memory which recalls "the light there almost solid," but not what canto it's in. Donald Gallup's extraordinary *Bibliography* of Pound often leads one in unexpectedly helpful directions (revised edition, 1983).

Several relatively compact guides combine glosses and interpretation. My *Guide to Ezra Pound's Selected Cantos* (1980) discusses the entire poem, with detailed commentary on the representative cantos and passages chosen by the poet in 1966 as "what he himself considers to provide the best introduction to the whole poem for those coming to it for the first time." *Selected Cantos* was published in slightly different versions by Faber (1967) and New Directions (1970). William Cookson's *A Guide to the Cantos of Ezra Pound* (1985) is excellent and efficient, The guide to *Selected Poems* by Peter Brooker (1979) supplies notes on the poems in *Personae* as well as on passages from the *Cantos* included in that volume.

All students eventually find their way to *Paideuma*, a journal devoted to Pound studies, which Terrell has been editing at the University of Maine at Orono since 1972. It has published often excellent, sometimes less than excellent, articles on all aspects of the *Cantos*, as well as texts of sources such as Baller's edition of *The Sacred Edict of K'ang Hsi*, of which Cantos 98–99 are a redaction. The pages of *Paideuma*, especially in recent years, reflect the spirited, usually collegial debates that go on in Pound studies. Representative of the best of *Paideuma* are two articles upon which I have drawn in chapter 2, Ian F. A. Bell's "Pound's Vortex: Shapes Ancient and Modern" (*Pai 10.2*) and Akiko Miyake's essay in *Pai* 10.3. The British journal *Agenda* has given special attention to Pound.

Hugh Kenner's dazzling *The Pound Era* (1971) is a classic, that rarity among critical studies, a book in itself *divertente*. Almost all later criticism follows Kenner, whether to read somewhat in his manner, or to argue, sometimes implicitly, against him. Donald Davie has two perceptive, original studies, the influential *Ezra Pound: Poet as Sculptor* (1965) and *Pound* (1975). An early book I continue to like very much is Christine Brooke-Rose's *A ZBC of Ezra Pound*, although readers demanding an "orderly" presentation should be warned that it works in a Poundian jumping-around way (which seems perfectly normal to me, but not to everyone). An excellent review of Pound's career, with four judicious chapters on the *Cantos*, is Michael Alexander's *The Poetic Achievement of Ezra Pound* (1979). Peter Makin's *Pound's Cantos* (1985) is thorough, paying more attention to the poetry than does most Pound criticism. Massimo Bacigalupo's *The Formèd Trace* (1980), concentrating on the later cantos, is generous with insights and ingenious research. Bacigalupo is particularly knowledgable on Pound's Italian background. James J. Wilhelm's *The Later Cantos of Ezra Pound*

(1977) is a more direct, enthusiastic reading of the difficult *Rock-Drill* and *Thrones*. The essays in Eva Hesse, ed., *New Approaches to Ezra Pound* (1969) are of a high standard.

In *The Genesis of Ezra Pound's Cantos* (1976), Ronald Bush goes far beyond what the title promises, although his emphasis is on the development of the poem in its early stages. Wendy Stallard Flory's *Ezra Pound and the Cantos: A Record of Struggle* (1980) is learned and original, taking a more biographical approach than do most of the books here recommended; her *The American Ezra Pound* (1989) explores the American roots of the poet's thought and politics. The religious–erotic elements in the poem are given judicious attention in Leon Surette's *The Light from Eleusis* (1979). In *The Tale of the Tribe* (1980), Michael André Bernstein is interested in the modern verse epic as a genre and in the problems that arise in the *Cantos* from conflicts between time and the timeless, history and myth. Marianne Korn's *Ezra Pound: Purpose/Form/Meaning* (1983) is short, well-informed, and lucid. George Bornstein's *The Postomantic Consciousness of Ezra Pound* (1977) is valuable. Marjorie Perloff places Pound within illuminating, often surprising "post-modern" contexts in *The Poetics of Indeterminacy* and her more recent *The Dance of the Intellect: Studies in the Poetry of the Pound Tradition* (1985).

On Pound's politics and its correlative anti-semitism, see Burton Hatlen's concise, well-balanced essay, "Ezra Pound and Fascism," in Marianne Korn, ed., *Ezra Pound and History* (1985). Recommended, too, is Cairns Craig, *Yeats, Eliot, Pound and the Politics of Poetry* (1982). See also William M. Chace, *The Political Identities of Ezra Pound and T. S. Eliot* (1973). A clear exposition of Pound's economic theories, but lacking any sophistication of analysis, is Earle Davis's *Vision Fugitive* (1968).

Recently, critics working from perspectives of modern critical theory have given attention to Pound. Among the best is Jean-Michel Rabaté's *Language, Sexuality and Ideology in Ezra Pound's Cantos* (1986). Contemporary approaches are reflected in *Ezra Pound: Tactics for Reading*, ed. Ian Bell (1982). Bell's *Critic as Scientist: The Modernist Poetics of Ezra Pound* (1981), is a fascinating investigation of the relations between science and poetry in the last hundred years. Christine Froula, in *To Write Paradise* (1984), argues for our acceptance of the errors in the text as inherent to its meaning. Although its subject is less the *Cantos* than Pound's prose, the insights of Kathryn V. Lindberg's *Reading Pound Reading: Modernism after Nietzsche* (1987) may readily be applied to the poem. Among theoretically informed writers, Lindberg best understands Pound's spirit, arguing against those who would have us believe, as one article claims, that Pound wishes to produce a monolithic meaning, "merely a commodity which can supposedly be passed on, traditionally."

More specialized studies exist than can be named here. For the reader who takes an interest, for example, in Pound's "Adams," his sense of the troubadour tradition and Provence, the Malatesta cantos, or the China cantos, there are, respectively: Frederick K. Sanders, *John Adams Speaking* (1975); Peter Makin, *Pound and Provence* (1978); Peter D'Epiro, *A Touch of Rhetoric* (1983); and John Nolde, *Blossoms from the East* (1983).

No full biography of Pound can be recommended warmly. The most straightforward, least sensational or journalistic, is Noel Stock, *The Life of Ezra Pound*, best consulted in its latest revision (1982). Of special interest is the fine memoir (1971) by the poet's daughter. Mary de Rachewiltz, which exists under two titles, *Ezra Pound, Father and Teacher: Discretions* and simply, *Discretions*.